WOMEN *of* FAITH

edited by
Mary S Sherrard

CHURCH *of* SCOTLAND
WOMAN'S GUILD

SAINT ANDREW PRESS
EDINBURGH

Published by
SAINT ANDREW PRESS
121 George Street, Edinburgh EH2 4YN
on behalf of the
CHURCH of SCOTLAND WOMAN'S GUILD

ISBN 0 86153 170 1

British Library Cataloguing in Publication Data
A catalogue record for this book
is available from the British Library

ISBN 0861531701

Design concept and cover by Mark Blackadder.
Cover photograph (background) by Paul Turner.
Photographs on pages 9, 54, 110 – by kind permission of
St Colm's Education Centre and College, Edinburgh.
Photograph on page 1 – by kind permission of St
Margaret's Chapel Guild.
Photograph on page 101 – by kind permission of Effie
Campbell.
Photograph on page 130 – by kind permission of the
Church of Scotland Department of World Mission and
Unity.
Illustrations on pages 4, 6, 16, 23, 30, 42, 44, 72, plus
other miscellaneous Guild details – from the Church
of Scotland Woman's Guild archive, Edinburgh.
Illustrations on pages 11 and 36 – from *Missionary
Heroines in Eastern Lands,* E R Pitman, S W Partridge
& Co Ltd: London.
Illustration on page 12 – by Michael Turnbull.
Illustration on page 31 – from *Scots Worthies: Their Lives
and Testimonies,* J A Wylie (ed),William Mackenzie:
London (1880).
Illustration on page 58 – from *Scottish Pictures,* S Green,
Religious Tract Society: London.

Typeset in 11.5/15 pt Garamond.
Printed and **bound** by Athenaeum Press Ltd, Newcastle
upon Tyne.

CONTENTS

CONTENTS

FOREWORD
by Dorothy Dalgliesh

'WE *walk by* FAITH,
not by SIGHT ...'

Faith is a very personal thing. It is the story of our discovery of God, and his love for us.

The seeds of faith have been sown by the faithful over the years, but it is only as we seek after truth for ourselves that the seed begins to grow and we find the truth of God's Word – seek and ye shall find.

This book contains the stories of some women whose lives have helped others to find meaningful faith. The stories are as varied as our paths to the knowledge of God, but the common thread through them all is the tale of the faithfulness of Almighty God to uphold his children through all the trials and tribulations of this life.

We will find much within this book which rings true to our own experience. We pray that sharing these stories will help and encourage all who seek to walk the path of faith.

~ AUGUST 1993 ~

INTRODUCTION
by Mary S Sherrard

Each session the Woman's Guild of the Church of Scotland invites its members to work to a theme. For 1991–92, the theme was 'Faith Works' and it was interpreted in different ways. It seemed that each of us had a story to tell, an illustration to give, of how faith had worked for and in us. Our faith was strengthened by what we saw in the lives of others – of women of faith.

As national office bearers travelled throughout Scotland – and England – they were encouraged and heartened and indeed moved by the stories of faith told to them.

At about this time we read that some women in the Presbyterian Church (USA) had produced a book, a collection of stories about women who had touched and influenced the lives of others.

Could we do something similar?

The Woman's Guild Communications Committee was very enthusiastic. So, in our newsletter of April 1992, we invited our members to write and tell us of women who had been an inspiration to them in their lives. We had no idea what the response would be. We were, after all, asking for a very personal insight.

This book is the result of our invitation. We offer it in tribute to those women who – usually unwittingly – have deepened the faith of others. It has certainly been a delight to correspond with those members and others who have taken up the challenge to write for us.

Some of the women written about in this book are known only in their own circle of family and friends. Others have influenced a great many women and their names are comparatively well known. Some stories come down to us from centuries past. Others are of today's generation.

All have been written about with love! Their faith has fanned the faith of others. The glory is to God.

We would like to thank *all* our contributors. And we are grateful too that Mamie Magnusson accepted our invitation to write accounts of two stalwarts of the Woman's Guild – Catherine Charteris and Mary Lamond. It is good to remember the work of these particular women – among so many others – whose work has helped progress the recognition of women's capabilities and contribution in Church and Society today.

A book such as this cannot be comprehensive. We have for the most part used the material submitted to us. The choice of subject has been left to our contributors. There are many women of faith who could, and should, be written about – but that must await a future edition!

Dorothy Dalgliesh was in office as National President of the Woman's Guild when this book was still a dream. To her, and to our General Secretary, Lorna Paterson, we offer thanks for unfailing interest, support and very practical help. And, as we have ventured into new realms, the encouragement of Saint Andrew Press has been warmly appreciated.

It fell to me, as the convener of the Communications Committee back in 1992, to head an editorial group of three. We have learned together and I take much pleasure in acknowledging the skill and work of my two colleagues, Marjorie Lawrie and Virginia Wilkie.

Our prayer is that this book will gladden the hearts of its readers and inspire women of faith today and tomorrow.

~ SEPTEMBER 1993 ~

SAINT MARGARET

QUEEN *of* SCOTLAND

In June 1993 a commemorative service was
held in Dunfermline Abbey to mark the
900th anniversary of the death of **Saint
Margaret**, Queen of Scotland [1045–
1093]. St Margaret's Shrine, where
she is buried, can be seen just outside the modern Abbey Church;
from medieval times it has been a
place of pilgrimage.

St Margaret's prayer life was the
essence of all she did. It is known
that she retreated to a cave in Dunfermline to meditate and pray. She
founded churches and chapels in
different parts of Scotland. The
Chapel in Edinburgh Castle bearing
her name was built for her by her
husband, Malcolm III of Scotland.

ST MARGARET'S
WINDOW,
ST MARGARET'S
CHAPEL,
EDINBURGH

In the book *Out of Silence* (by Mamie
Magnusson, Edinburgh 1987) we read of
the 'Guild of St Margaret in the Kirk of St
Nicholas', probably the oldest Woman's
Guild in Scotland. This Guild, which was
founded in Aberdeen in 1882 by Revd

James Cooper, took as its motto – 'By love serve one another. Watch and pray'. The life of St Margaret is depicted in the stained glass windows of the church.

Five years later, Dr Charteris was to base the constitution of the newly formed national Woman's Guild on the Guild of St Margaret in Aberdeen.

Today many churches continue to take the name of St Margaret.

Who was ST MARGARET?

It is certainly a romantic story. Margaret was a Saxon Princess of the Wessex royal house, born 1045 in Hungary where her father was in exile, and brought up in the Court of Edward the Confessor. To escape from the danger of the Norman Conquest in 1066, Margaret took a ship bound for the Continent. It was driven northwards by adverse winds, eventually landing on the south coast of Fife. Here she was received very hospitably by the Scottish King, Malcolm Canmore.

This was a great event in our history – coming as it did at our emergence as a nation which until then was a patchwork of petty princedoms. Spiritually, too, the lamps of the ancient Culdee Church and the

Columban faith that followed it 500 years later had grown dim. Scotland was rough – so perforce was the King.

Margaret – beautiful, educated, capable, virtuous – came like a bright light into a dark world. The King, unpolished but good-hearted, was entranced. Whether she equally returned his love is uncertain, but she believed that this was her destiny and in her early twenties she became Malcolm's Queen, bearing him two daughters and six sons. Together they guided Scotland into the mainstream of European religion and culture of the time.

Not only was Margaret constant in her faith, but diligent in its practice – releasing slaves, feeding the poor, founding new churches, setting up what must have been the first Woman's Work Party (men excluded, even the King!) and setting in motion the social work of the Church.

Alas, both the King and Queen died tragically in 1093 – he defending his be-loved realm against the Normans at the Battle of Alnwick – she of sickness shortly afterwards.

~ ADELAIDE COGHILL ~

[*"who was ST MARGARET?' was taken from the magazine of St Margarets Parish Church, Glenrothes, Fife.*]

CATHERINE ANDERSON CHARTERIS

The LAUNCH *of the* WOMAN'S GUILD

In the torrent of tributes that followed the death of Dr Archibald Charteris [1835–1908], his widow was referred to as 'his true yolk-fellow and loving helpmeet'. It might sound like the typical period way of saying that Mrs Charteris had been a good wife, faithful and true to the vows she had made at their wedding fifty years earlier, to 'love, honour and obey ... till death us do part'.

But KATIE ANDERSON CHARTERIS [1837–1918] elder daughter of the Lord Provost of Aberdeen, was much more than just the dutiful appendage to one of the most illustrious churchmen in the history of the Church of Scotland. When Dr Charteris met Catherine Morice Anderson he realised that he had found a young woman who embodied everything he had envisaged for the future of women in the Church.

Dr Charteris was the founder of the

CATHERINE ANDERSON CHARTERIS

Woman's Guild and the Order of Deaconesses, pioneer of the Church's vast social
work programme at home and abroad, the
man who was to give women the chance to
have their say, long before women's suffrage.
Katie became his inspiration and his justifi-
cation for continuing the long battle against
powerful opposition to persuade the all-
male General Assembly of the Church of
Scotland to harness the untapped fervour of
women in order to lift his beloved Church
out of the doldrums brought about by the
Great Disruption of 1843.

Katie had a faith to match his own. She
was highly intelligent and well educated,
able to hold her own in any conversation,
exchange repartee with her father's visitors
and express her opinions with an informal
friendliness unusual at a time when women's
opinions were seldom offered or invited.

She was to need her sense of humour for
the life that awaited her after her marriage.
Not for her the genteel chit-chat over the
manse tea-cups at their first charge in
Glasgow's Great Western Road. She was too
busy leading forays of West End matrons to
Port Dundas to dispense food and clothing
and run Sunday Schools, mothers' meetings
and children's outings as part of her husband's experiment in Christian social work.

When he collapsed from overwork, and

The ORIGINAL LIST *of* MEMBERS *of the* NEWLY-FORMED
WOMAN'S GUILD (*in* MRS CHARTERIS'S *own* HANDWRITING)

when ill-health forced him to accept a chair
at Edinburgh University, she did everything she could to take the burden off his
shoulders. When he embarked on a scheme
of social work among the slums of the
Pleasance, she had teams of volunteers keeping a detailed register of each family's
health, welfare and every need which could
be met out of church donations. She ran
what must have been Edinburgh's first
social club for working folk in a first-floor
flat in the Lawnmarket.

She was in the thick of the eruption of
activity which followed the launch of the
Woman's Guild in 1887. She became its

first president in 1895. And as the first editor of the Woman's Guild magazine, she tirelessly rallied her troops to organise country markets for the poor of the cities, to make bandages for fisher lassies, to send hospital equipment to India, to equip and maintain the Deaconess Hospital in Edinburgh, to set up homes for alcoholics.

She had no children of her own, but she brought up a nephew for ten years of her busy life.

If she had a favourite project, it was the Home-House for the children of missionaries. She would visit them regularly, bring them to her home at weekends and send them Christmas presents until the day she died in 1918.

Perhaps the best thing that Archibald Charteris did during a life of outstanding achievement was to find and marry Katie Anderson.

~ MAMIE MAGNUSSON ~

ANNIE
HUNTER
SMALL

The PRACTICAL SAINT

Born at Redding near Falkirk, **ANNIE HUNTER SMALL** [1857–1945] spent her early years in Poona, where her father, Revd John Small, was a missionary of the Free Church of Scotland. At 19, after school in England, she returned to Poona as a missionary, gaining a deep love and understanding of India and extensive knowledge of the work. Since fragile health dogged her all her life she was forced to leave India in 1892.

Annie's return to Scotland coincided with the decision made by the Woman's Foreign Mission Committee recommending that specialised training was needed for women who offered themselves for missionary service. She was the obvious person to pioneer this work. So, in 1894, the Women's Missionary Training Institute (later St Colm's College) opened in Edinburgh. Annie was principal of the Institute until 1913 and responsible for its growth. With its blend of study, practical work and worship, in a residential setting, it attracted students from many countries. It soon became a model of excellence for other churches, and was commended by the 1910 Edinburgh World Missionary Conference.

Annie had great gifts and wide interests. She was no academic, but her impact as a teacher of the Bible was profound. She was respected by scholars for her knowledge of India and its religions, and moved easily among the great men of her time. Widely read, she wrote graphically and with grace, from stories of Indian life to devotional studies of the Gospels and Psalms. But music was a special joy – she published an innovative Missionary hymnbook, which included Indian and Chinese tunes.

ANNIE HUNTER SMALL

Annie Small inspired devotion – each student was cherished as an individual with potential and talents, encouraged to maintain a lively interest in the wider world while learning to live in a community. Her ability to relate to younger people continued into old age, when she was still in demand as a speaker at student conferences. Those who knew her, speak of her common sense and selfless humility, a person radiating energy, joy and goodness.

For her entire life, Annie Small was open to new ideas. The College was a place of experiment in curriculum and worship, and of ecumenical encounter; yet it all was solidly based on the sense of being part of a historic succession. Her devotion to the island of Iona (she is credited with drawing Revd George MacLeod's attention to Iona, where he rebuilt the Abbey and founded the Iona Community) and its Celtic past, her re-discovery of ancient Scottish prayers, her use of the Psalms in daily worship, all reflected the way she sought the roots of her religious heritage. She also believed other races equally had their own tradition, and therefore the Christian missionary must humbly seek to understand the history and religious beliefs of those among whom they worked. Secure in her own faith, Annie Small did not fear dialogue with those of other religions.

For this 'woman of faith', prayer and worship were central. Her father had taught the necessity of daily personal prayer and this she always emphasised. She also introduced her students to the unsuspected riches of corporate worship. Daily worship in the chapel she loved so much became the essential and memorable core of College life.

Annie Small's influence spread far beyond the College and is still felt in the Church today. Her name lives on in the Annie

Small Centre attached to St Colm's College
(now designated by the General Assembly
of the Church of Scotland as the Church's
Education Centre and College).

Annie Hunter Small always maintained
that the greatest function of a missionary, at
home or abroad, was 'to reveal the
Christian life'. She was rightly described as
'a saint, but a very practical one'.

~ ISABEL LUSK ~

A NINETEENTH CENTURY MISSIONARY
discusses the BIBLE *with a* HINDU LADY

ELSIE
MAUD
INGLIS

The ARDENT SUFFRAGIST

The faith of **Dr ELSIE INGLIS** [1864–1917] was built into the fabric of her life. Even in the thick of war, she always carried her book of daily devotions as part of her personal survival kit which included her pen, watch, stethoscope and a paint box. These articles can still be seen in the Imperial War Museum in London.

So, who was Elsie Inglis? Well, during World War I, Elsie was a household name – due to her work in organising the Scottish Women's Hospitals Committee to send Units to France, Serbia and Russia.

DR ELSIE
INGLIS

Nowadays her name is chiefly associated with the maternity hospital in Edinburgh which was established in her memory. Sadly, it was recently closed down.

Seventy-five years after Elsie's death, it is perhaps difficult to appreciate the significance of her work. She was an ardent suffragist who was, however, opposed to the aggressive methods of the suffragettes.

In fact, it was through her involvement with
the suffrage movement that the idea of Units
staffed entirely by women (doctors, nurses,
orderlies and drivers) became a reality.

Elsie herself was indefatigable, an
enthusiastic public speaker whose efforts
helped to raise enough money in three
months to send the first all-female Medical
Units to war-torn France in November
1914. Other Units soon followed. In April
1915, Elsie herself set out for Serbia, where
she and her colleagues worked tirelessly,
enduring the horrors and dangers of war
without thought for themselves.

There are many descriptions of the
privations endured by the women, but all
the accounts speak highly of Elsie Inglis –
of her devotion to duty, her own high standards and similar expectations of others,
her compassion for those in need of care,
and her courage and fearless persistence in
the face of government red tape.

Despite the fact that she may have been
difficult to work with, Elsie Inglis com-
manded respect for her authority and was a
much loved leader who inspired those under
her direction.

Elsie seems to have been a very private
person who did not generally find it easy
to speak about matters of faith, but it is
undeniable that her motivation was truly

Christian. In conditions where church-going was impossible, she would read the service to the Unit each Sunday, as well as attend to her own private devotions every day throughout her life.

Her thoughtfulness for the spiritual needs of her patients, and her understanding of the deep religious feelings of the Russians in particular, showed itself in the provision of ikons for the four wards in her hospital. She characteristically felt that she could justify the expense of 45 shillings by explaining to the fund-raising committee the importance of showing the people that 'one has sympathy for them'.

Elsie's childhood in India, as part of a large and loving family, meant that her Christian principles were instilled at a very early age. She was particularly close to her father, an enlightened man, who encouraged her to train as a doctor at a time when it was difficult for women to do so.

Most of her life was spent in Edinburgh, surrounded by her family for whom she had great affection and a particular rapport with the younger members.

Her interests were many and varied, like her work. Outwith her war duties, she ran her own practice which included a small hospice for women; she acted as surgeon at the Bruntsfield Hospital for women; she even lectured on midwifery and, early in her career, established a medical school for women. All these activities, combined with socialising and regular church attendance, meant that each day was very full. Time-keeping, however, was not her strong point apparently. She was invariably late for supper!

Elsie's main concern was for the poor families in her care and she was a dedicated and much-loved doctor, giving practical help in imaginative and often unconventional ways. For example, a written prescription might not specify pills, but require the patient to eat regular meals, go to bed early and take an interest in the church!

When the Great War broke out, Dr Inglis was 50 years old. After such an active life, the years of war work took their toll on her health and she returned from Russia in November 1917, a very sick woman. Some-how she survived the dreadful journey to Newcastle, where she spent the last day of her life, comforted by her sisters and the words of Scripture in her little book of daily devotions.

At the age of 53, Dr Elsie Inglis died, not only a heroine of war, but also a woman of faith, of courage and of vision.

A colleague wrote: 'She was the truest and most faithful friend a woman ever had'.

~ RUTH FORBES ~

MARY
LAMOND

Reorganising the GUILD

MARY LAMOND was a remarkable woman who devoted her entire adult life to the Church of Scotland. She was an outstanding product of the minor revolution which hit the Church in the 1880s with the establishment of the Woman's Guild and the Order of Deaconesses.

Many people doubted whether women could cope with the demands of organisation and leadership which had always been the province of men. It took women like Mary Lamond to show the world that women could cope, and cope wonderfully. There seemed to be no job which she was not capable of taking on.

MARY
LAMOND

First she trained for the highest calling available to a woman at that time, that of Deaconess. She was 'set apart' at a special service in Morningside Church, Edinburgh, on 1 April 1894, and very soon she was training deaconesses as assistant superintendent at their training house in Edinburgh.

By 1911 she had become superintendent, and only relinquished that post after becoming president of the Woman's Guild in 1920 (she had already been its secretary for six years by then, and before that she had been editor of the Guild magazine).

Now she concentrated her considerable intellectual, organisational and leadership skills on making the Guild an even greater force, completely reorganising the whole set-up. Whereas hundreds of Guild branches had been loosely grouped into a few large regions, with only one representative from each region attending the Guild Central Committee meetings in Edinburgh, Mary Lamond divided the regions into smaller groups of branches based on the Church Presbyteries, with every Presbyterial Council sending a representative to Edinburgh. Now the Central Committee was swelled by representatives from every part of Scotland, making it a real 'parliament' of the Guild.

During the Depression years which followed the General Strike of 1926, Mary Lamond inspired her Guildswomen to ever greater efforts to ease the plight of the poor and sick. That was the year in which the Guild of Deaconesses pledged to supply the Deaconess Hospital with bed linen for the next three years. In one year – 1928 – a single Guild in Campbeltown knitted 40 pairs of stockings for the Bootless Fund, provided clothing for 111 families and an orphanage in Musselburgh, and supplied a local deaconess with clothes and groceries.

Mary Lamond next turned her attention to training Guild members in public speaking and voice-production, so that there would always be a supply of good speakers to go round branches, rallying the troops.

Meanwhile she was busy masterminding the greatest achievement of her career – the merger of the Woman's Guild of the Church of Scotland with the women's organisations of the United Free Church in the reunion of the churches in 1929. At the historic union celebration, before a special Assembly of the highest churchmen in the land, Mary Lamond was the only woman speaker: 'Miss Lamond brilliantly vindicated women's place in the Church,' said the official report.

So great was the increase in Guild membership that in 1932 – her final year as president – Mary Lamond had to hire Edinburgh's Usher Hall for the first annual conference of the largest organisation of women in the land. Then she retired and went home to study Hebrew, so that she could read the Psalms in the original.

Mary Lamond died in 1949.

~ MAMIE MAGNUSSON ~

MARY ELIZABETH HALDANE

The STRENGTH *of the* LORD

MARY ELIZABETH HALDANE of Cloan, as she entered her centenary year, wrote to Randall Davidson when he was Archbishop of Canterbury (1903–1928), saying:

> *The nearer I approach eternity, the more satisfied and happy that life seems to become. I do not know why: but I think it is owing to the great realisation of the Sovereign Will of God, over-ruling everything and leaving us helpless in His hands. We rest as little helpless infants in His arms.*

And to a young minister called Dr James S Stewart – later to become the world-renowned preacher and author – at that time starting out in his first charge at Auchterarder, she gave this as a text for his daily living: 'I will go forth in the strength of the Lord'.

~ PEGGY BIRKBECK ~

MARJORIE
PENMAN

The word 'lady' conjures up many images, but the subject of this particular portrait truly embodied all the high standards of that word.

MARJORIE PENMAN lived in a small place in Midlothian. Her presence there brought a sense of joy to those who shared her neighbourhood. By the economics of her day, she was well off and lived in a large house, but this did not set her apart from the other church folk who came from all walks of life.

Being active with time and money in the local Church of Scotland was not her entire life of faith, however. Marjorie viewed her wealth as given in trust and she was determined to use it wisely and with care. When, for example, she realised that some of the shares she had bought were in concerns whose employees were asked to work on Sunday, her contributions were promptly withdrawn.

In the course of her life, she met the needs of many children who were without food, clothes or the chance of a holiday. But it was the way in which she gave that made her so special – for the children were shown her love. The food was served at her own dinner table in a gracious manner and each child felt honoured. As if each child were her own, the new clothing was chosen and tried on in the best shops in Edinburgh. Marjorie and her friends even took the children with them on their own holidays.

No physical remembrance of Marjorie Penman remains with me after sixty years, but the spiritual attributes never dim. Her faith was alive with love.

In 1990 a painting of two little girls by Marjorie Penman's brother appeared in the National Gallery of Scotland. She was one of the girls.

~ HOPE BAKER ~

HELEN
WILSON

The MISSIONARY NURSE

In 1961 the television programme 'This is your Life' featured **HELEN WILSON** [1891–1978], a Church of Scotland missionary nurse who had spent 40 years in the Far East.

The highlight of the evening was the joyful reunion with a young man, fully recovered from tuberculosis of the spine, whom Helen had nursed in Hong Kong.

Helen's sympathy for disadvantaged people had its origins in her own life when, as a small child in Aberdeen, she was badly disfigured by burning. She was determined to overcome this handicap and the resulting shyness which had caused her to leave school at 15 years old to train as a dress-maker.

At 21, Helen had a conversion experience and felt that she wanted to do something useful with her life. She was dissuaded from training as a nurse because of her disfigurement, so Helen pursued her overwhelming desire to learn more about the Bible. She therefore trained at the Bible Training Institute in Glasgow, thanks to the generosity of one of her brothers. She also undertook mid-wifery training before offering herself for service as a missionary.

In 1920 she was sent as an evangelist to Ichang in China, but for the next seven years most of her time was spent helping to run the Women's Mission Hospital. As a result of this experience, Helen Wilson returned to Scotland to train as a nurse in the Deaconess Hospital in Edinburgh where, at the age of 40, she pass-ed the course with flying colours.

HELEN
WILSON

Then it was back to China, where life was becoming difficult in the wake of the Japanese invasion of North China and the resulting influx of patients – victims of the war.

Following later internment by the Jap-anese, the missionaries, including Helen, were due to be repatriated early in 1942. But by the time they reached the West, the last British ship had left. Helen and the others remained in Shanghai, caring for people there until the war ended.

In 1945 it was finally possible to return to Ichang. A Chinese doctor, a man called Dr Wei, had somehow managed to keep things going while the hospital was being occupied by the Japanese. He even managed to salvage some of the equipment.

Life was not easy after the war, but Helen continued to provide medical care.

However, with the coming of the communist regime, missionaries were no longer welcome. Helen and a colleague – Dr Macrae – were put on trial on a trumped-up charge. Throughout her difficulties, Helen's faith kept her going until eventually the two were deported to Hong Kong.

When Helen was near retiring age, she was so moved by the desperate plight of the 20,000 refugees whom she saw on a visit to Rennie's Mill Camp in Hong Kong that she persuaded the Church of Scotland to allow her to stay and work among them. There she helped to establish a clinic in a small rudimentary bamboo hut, with little equipment. From there the work grew, as the nurses worked to control the widespread malnutrition and the enormous problem of tuberculosis.

Perhaps Helen's finest work was done amongst those Chinese refugees. It certainly attracted the attention of, amongst others, the World Council of Churches, which awarded a grant towards a new clinic which was opened in 1954.

Despite suffering ill-health, Helen continued to work at the Camp and was able to use the facilities of the new Haven of Hope Sanatorium with its 105 beds for tuberculosis patients for the last three years of her time there.

When she finally retired, aged 68, it was in the knowledge that her care for the Chinese people, coupled with her personal faith and persistence in times of difficulties, resulted in many being brought to Christ and healed of their disease.

But that is not the end of the story! Six years after she retired, Helen married the Revd Dr Forbes Tocher with whom she had worked in Ichang. Her remaining years were spent back home in the North East of Scotland.

Helen Wilson, woman of faith, this is your life!

~ RUTH FORBES ~

NETTA
FORMAN *

Reaching out ...

NETTA FORMAN [1910–1992] was born in
Greenock and grew up there, and in St
Andrews, in an evangelical Christian home.
While attending St Andrews university, she
was influenced by the short week-day services and by the branch of the Inter-Varsity
Fellowship of Evangelical Unions. She began
to ask critical questions about theology and
earned the nick-name 'the Left Wing'. But
despite intellectual disagreements, she was
able to enjoy fellowship of spirit with all.

After graduation, Netta felt herself called to serve with the South Africa General
Mission which was at that time looking for
someone to pioneer the education of girls
in an outlying area of what is now known
as Zambia. So, after a year of study at
Glasgow's Bible Training Institute, she
began her work in Zambia in 1936, at the
mission station in Mukinge.

At first she worked hard to learn the
language. Indeed, she was so successful that
she later produced school books in Zambesi
and took an active part in Bible translation.

Netta then recruited twelve pupils, aged 10–14, to make up the first class of the first girls' school in the district. By the time she left, the school had developed its full range of classes with girls from other districts attending the upper classes. A start had been made in training women teachers in Zambia.

Christian worship and teaching were central to the life of the school, with the keeping of the main festivals of the Christian year a special feature. Netta later said that it was at Mukinge that Easter came alive for her, witnessing it celebrated year by year by some who did so for the first time. The school was later chosen by the Zambian Government as the centre for girls' secondary education for the whole of the North West Province.

During Netta's time in Zambia, many benefitted from her quiet, wise and godly influence. She was well-loved by her missionary colleagues, despite her differing theological views.

When she came to leave Mukinge, one of her African workers said, 'Who will laugh with us now you are going?'

One of the first pupils commented sadly, 'We call you mother [a term of respect], but you are more like our big sister'.

In later years, Netta was heartened to learn of the Christian witness and service

many of her former pupils were giving in
the developing life of Zambia.

In the early 1950s she began to feel that
she was being called to move on. In her
spare time she studied for and gained a
Diploma in Theology. In 1955 she moved
to Krobo Training College, in what is now
Ghana, as a Kirk missionary serving with
the local Presbyterian church. There Netta
revelled in the richness of Ghana's history,
culture, church life and people.

Krobo had a high reputation and it was
not long before Netta was appointed as its
Principal. She guided the College well
through the heady and sometimes difficult
days of the newly independent Ghana. Worship in chapel played a big part in college
life, with imaginative use of music and
drama. She certainly drew out the best from
students and staff alike, especially her
Ghanaian tutors. Delighting in her share of
teaching, Netta said afterwards, 'Admin-
istration was my job, but teaching was my
besetting sin'.

Outside the College, Netta won the
confidence of Church leaders and ministers.
She was well respected in the Conference of
Training College Principals where she worked happily with individuals from different
denominations. She kept in touch with
many of these people even after she retired.

In 1969 Netta returned to St Andrews, but retirement did not come easily to her. One year later, she was asked by the Young Women's Christian Association to work with Asian immigrants in Dundee.

It is hard to imagine a better person for such work than Netta, with her capacity for making friends across differences of culture and religious tradition. A small centre was established and in her hands the work prospered, forming the basis for the Dundee International Women's Centre now situated in Lyon Street.

She made many friends among the Dundee Asians, maintaining contact with some of them for years after her work ended. The work there was her first real encounter with the great religious faiths of Asia and it led her to a clearer conviction about God's dealings with people of different faiths.

Netta Forman showed a sensitive interest in people of every kind, establishing a rapport with many in the things of the Spirit. Her deep Christian faith continued to develop all through her life and in her writing she reflects on 'all the ways that the Lord her God had led her'. She was someone who knew how to live joyfully under the love of God revealed in Jesus.

~ ANNE BENNET ~

[*Based upon material provided by Colin Forrester-Paton.*]

Grisell Baillie

LADY GRISELL BAILLIE

A MODEL CHRISTIAN

'She was a model Christian, bright, cheerful and joyous, carrying sunshine and gladness wherever she went.'

This tribute paid to **Lady GRISELL BAILLIE** from the pulpit of Bowden Kirk by Revd Alfred MacFarlane on Sunday 27 December 1891, a few days after she died, was well-deserved. Great-great-granddaughter of Grisell Baillie, the seventeenth century heroine of Polwarth Kirk, she was born at Mellerstain near Kelso where she was brought up by her mother who was a committed Christian.

After her husband's early death, Mrs Baillie with her son, Major Robert Baillie, and her daughter, Lady Grisell, moved to Eildon Hall from where a long association with Bowden Kirk began. Major Baillie was ordained to the eldership and he and his sister 'formed plans for the spiritual welfare of all amongst whom they lived'. For nearly fifty years they gave of their time, their talents and their means to the parish with a special interest in young people. For all that time they conducted the Sabbath School in Bowden Kirk. They also regularly attended the annual examination of the children in the village school which was conducted by the minister of Bowden and another representative of the Presbytery, the main subject being Bible Knowledge.

In 1858 they move to Maxpoffle, a small estate near the kirk, and in 1864 to Dryburgh from which they drove early every Sunday morning to Bowden to teach, pray and sing with the children. Thereafter they attended the morning and afternoon services, leaving for home at 3 p.m. For both, regular worship in church was of paramount importance.

GRISELL BAILLIE – *the* 'SEVENTEENTH CENTURY HEROINE *of* POLWARTH KIRK'

In this respect Lady Grisell's generosity was shown once more. As the journey by foot from Dryburgh by the bridge over the Tweed at Mertoun was long and tiring, she built at her own expense a suspension bridge over the river at Dryburgh to make it easier for people to walk to church.

After Major Baillie's death in 1888 she moved to The Holmes at St Boswells where she spent the last years of her life.

Lady Grisell's energies were spent not

merely in Bowden, Mertoun and Earlston, in which parishes she had resided at various times, but in the wider work of the Church at home and abroad. She was one of the founder members of the Zenana Mission (now Inter-Serve, Scotland) which provided medical care by women doctors for Muslim women in India. In 1878, having read a pamphlet on Temperance entitled *The National Sin*, she was so deeply affected that she immediately gave up the habit of drinking a small glass of white wine with her meals and devoted herself to the cause of total abstinence. She also began to organise a Band of Hope in Newtown and later founded a branch in Bowden.

In Bowden Kirk on 9 December 1888 Lady Grisell was commissioned as the first Deaconess of the Church of Scotland—'a day as bright and cloudless as her own spirit' (Bowden Parish leaflet).

When the Woman's Guild held its first conference in Edinburgh in 1891, Lady Grisell delivered the opening address 'in ringing tones of a silver trumpet'. Shortly afterwards, just before Christmas, she died and was buried at Mellerstain.

In Edinburgh the Lady Grisell Baillie Hospital was erected in commemoration of her life and work – later called the Deaconess Hospital. In Bowden a new Communion

Table was gifted in her memory and was used until after the final restoration of the Kirk in 1909. That memorial table now stands in the church at Gangtok, Sikkim, in the Eastern Himalayas.

Although Lady Grisell had conducted women's meetings for many years in the parish, it was not until after her death that the Woman's Guild was formed in Bowden on 15 May 1892 with Mrs Allardyce as its first President.

Since her death she has been honoured on two recent occasions. On 26 May 1960, Miss Alison Cunningham, who was the Youth Organiser for the Synod of Merse and Teviotdale, was commissioned there as a Deaconess of the Church of Scotland. In 1988 a special service was held in the Church to mark the centenary of Lady Grisell's commissioning. The service was conducted by Alison Cunningham.

In her biography, written by her sister Lady Ashburton, many of Lady Grisell's addresses and prayers are printed. Like her, the women of the Church of Scotland might use this petition:

'O Lord Our God, grant us the work of Thy Spirit in our hearts that we may become more and more like Our Great Example. Amen.'

~ JESSIE MACDONALD ~

A SIMPLE
FAITH

The misty isles of the West Coast seem to have brought forth men and women of keen clearness of mind and faith. The folk there won a rich simplicity of faith and practice from the poverty and harshness of their surroundings.

An elderly Hebridean woman said to a visiting minister: 'When I am in my little house and stare at the four walls, there will visit me many a troubling thought. But when they over-vex me, I open my door and stare at the sun and the sea. Then I feel I am gazing at eternity and all my dark thoughts are fled'.

~ PEGGY BIRKBECK ~

CATHERINE SINCLAIR

A USEFUL PEN

CATHERINE SINCLAIR [1800–1864] was a woman of action as well as studious habits, ready to take up social causes which deterred many of her sex. She was an authoress of bestsellers who sought and found causes in Edinburgh where help was most required.

For example, she introduced cooking-depots in the city where, for a paltry sum, tradesmen and folk on the poverty line could get a full meal. And university students with scant income were catered for with the setting up of a kitchen especially for them. She also instigated the first public fountain 'for man and beast' to quench their thirst, and cab-stands to provide shelter for drivers.

Catherine worked ceaselessly to better conditions for the poor, using money she earned from her writing. From this skill she desired neither fame nor profit, only usefulness. Her personal philosophy came from these words: 'Of all the paper I have blotted, I have written nothing without the intention of some good'.

~ PEGGY BIRKBECK ~

ISOBEL
GUNN

MOTHER *of the* PEOPLE

ISOBEL GUNN [1875–1932] graduated in medicine, married the Revd George M Kerr and, together, they started a primitive leper settlement in Nizamabad, India.

At that time a wonderful discovery was made. Leprosy might not be incurable! Oil from the fruit of the Chaulmoogra tree was proving beneficial to the leper. The 'Mother of the People', as Isobel was widely and affectionately called by the neglected mass of Indian lepers, said, 'I feel like a traveller who sees a light at the end of a long dark tunnel. A new era in Christ's ministry to lepers has dawned'.

News that there was hope for lepers spread like wildfire. Afflicted people streamed into Nizamabad, ready to trust their doctor-*dorasani*, eager to receive the prick of her hypodermic needle.

Isobel watched in wonder as a patient sat up after a routine massage, and sobbed for joy, 'Madam! madam! I was a leper and could feel nothing. Today I felt your hands all over me!'

The 'Leper Home' became known as 'Hospital' and the segregation camp was transformed into a curative centre. God's grace, working through medical science, had conquered.

~ PEGGY BIRKBECK ~

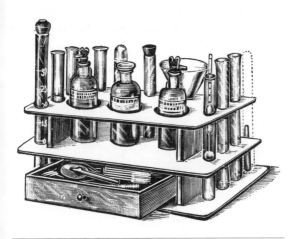

The
BLESSINGS
of GOD

A poor Highland woman, unable to read or write, derived great compensation from observing nature. She noted how the frail petals of the flax or lint-bell unfolded in the sunshine and closed when its rays were withdrawn.

Ignorant of many things she may well have been, but one gift was her's indeed – the capacity to understand, accept and love the blessings of God, from the 'inestimable gift' of his Son to the least flower that bloomed in her path.

On applying to her minister to be admitted to the Lord's Supper, her ignorance of basic doctrines was so palpable that she was deemed unfit to become a communicant.

The minister told her as kindly as he could. She simply said: 'Aweel, sir, aweel. But I ken ae thing – as the lint-bell opens to the sun, so does my heart to the Lord Jesus!'

~ PEGGY BIRKBECK ~

A TRIUMPHANT FAITH

A close friend fought a triumphant battle with cancer in the last five years of her life. Her courage and faith were challenging and faith-giving for myself and for many of her friends.

Like other sufferers, she dreaded possible physical pain, separation from her husband. and the prospect of death. As our manse was at the seaside, she spent some time with us when she was convalescing from surgery.

One morning, she told us later, as she looked out over the sea from her bedroom window, fear and depression swept over her, and she wept. Then she remembered the lines of a chorus she had learned as a child. As she repeated it over and over again, the words began to help her:

Wide, wide as the ocean,
High as the heaven above,
Deep, deep as the deepest sea
Is my Saviour's love.
I, though so unworthy,
Still am a child of His care,

For His word teaches me
That His love reaches me
Everywhere.

The many hymns she knew by heart
were of great help to her in the years that
followed. During her deep-ray treatment in
hospital she would repeat to herself the lines:

Let the healing streams abound,
Make and keep me pure within.

My friend and her husband were honest
with each other about their fears. They faced
the future together and so were able to support each other. My friend had a deep longing to be an equal partner with her husband,
and to care for him for all his earthly life.
One of the hardest things she did was place
him unreservedly in God's hands, and trust
for his future welfare without her.

Right to the end she played to win, and
the hymn 'Fight the good fight with all thy
might' was a constant source of encouragement. She certainly fought the good fight
against evil, both of body and spirit.

Those who visited her were amazed to
find a home, not of sickness and darkness,
but of joy and light. She died peacefully
and trustfully. Her faith had triumphed
over fear and pain.

~ LORNA LAIRD ~

EVELYN
SLOAN

The FAMILY
of the CHURCH

> *And my prayer for the ministry just
> beginning is that God will open the windows
> of heaven and pour down such a blessing
> that there will not be room to contain it.*

So ended the liveliest speech at the
Induction Social, the speech made by the
President of the Woman's Guild. It was
typical of EVELYN SLOAN [1889–1978] that
she could follow humour with seriousness,
using words of the Bible naturally, commit-
ting herself to pray and looking to God with
trust and hope.

She seldom spoke about herself and
probably few of those listening knew that
she was an early woman graduate, or that
she had been Ladies Golf Champion of
South India. More may have known that
when her widowed brother appealed to her
for help, she came over to run the household and to help bring up four children,
staying there for many years.

Her attitude was that her life was at
God's disposal and she coped with what

came her way with a twinkle in her eye.

Young people loved her – her 'adopted family', and later *their* families, and those who started coming to her church. She was so interested in them, particularly in their romances – invitations to tea provided the chance for both laughter and a sharing of hopes for the future.

Was it coincidence that several of her young friends became ministers or mission-aries? Certainly these men and women, still serving God, remember Evelyn Sloan as a very special person.

Although she herself faced life positively, Evelyn had enormous sympathy for the troubles of others. In her own life she had known grief at a favourite brother's death during the Great War, and also the slow fatal illness of one of her adopted family.

She was also sensitive enough to feel for those in need at home and abroad. The Woman's Guild minutes of the 1930s and 40s show her enthus-iasm for getting involved.

On one occasion, when the Committee wanted a lighter, more entertaining syllabus, she asked for a missionary meeting. Not surprisingly she had to organise it her-self. She liked a challenge and so she organised a film, a talk and a play (with her own costumes, words and direction), providing a fascinating and thought-provoking evening.

The most important thing for Evelyn Sloan was to know Christ as her personal Saviour and to walk obediently with him. This is what she longed for, for others. Therefore prayer was central to her life – three times a day, at the weekly Prayer Meeting, and in response to need. Six weeks before her death, she continued to attend the Prayer Meeting conscientiously and church twice on Sunday. By this time she was 89.

When her final illness came, although she was very weak, she asked the minister about his family. She had no complaints, but confided her longing to be at the Prayer Meeting on Saturday. By Saturday she was closer still to her Lord.

It is now 15 years since she died, but people still speak of her. She walked with God.

~ JOY PHILIP ~

MARY
MACNICOL

A HEART *given to* CHRIST

Dr MARY MACNICOL [1871–1962] was a
pioneering Scot, whose friendship I valued.
Her lively sparkling faith, after a lifetime
of commitment to the Lord, was a great
inspiration and challenge to me. I still
treasure the card on which she wrote for me
these lines from Walt Whitman:

> *Sail forth ... steer for the deep waters only,*
> *Restless, O Soul, exploring.*
> *I with Thee, and Thou with me.*
> *For we are bound where mariner has not*
>   *dared to go,*
> *And we will risk the ship, ourselves, and all.*
> *A daring joy, but safe! Are they not all the*
>   *seas of God?*

These words were certainly the theme
of Mary Macnicol's life. Her Christian

experience started in her childhood in India, when, at an evangelical meeting, all who wished to give their hearts to Christ were asked to stand. She did so, standing on a seat in order to be seen. It was a real experience which was to last a lifetime.

When she finished school, in 1889, Mary resolved to become a medical missionary. She was a niece of Elsie Inglis, the pioneering woman doctor, so she knew the difficulties that lay ahead for her in her chosen profession. She was one of the first students in the Medical College for Women which opened in Edinburgh in 1890, and the first woman to pass the final examination with distinction.

Then followed years of devoted medical missionary work in India, eventually with her husband, Dr Malcolm Macnicol. Sadly for them, they lost their 17 month-old son after a day's illness, probably sun-stroke. She recalled her bitter resentment at this loss until one day the words of the 23rd Psalm came home to her: 'Goodness and mercy all my life shall surely follow me'.

In her later years, despite failing sight, Mary never lost her light touch and sense of humour. She once told her family: 'You know, it's quite a good thing I'm going blind. I was beginning to lose my memory, and now I *have* to remember where I put things!'

After a dispute with her daughter on one occasion, Mary was downcast, until she remembered, ' … it's not too late at eighty to start all over again – even if it's just for a fortnight!'

Just before Mary Macnicol died, her last words to her son were, 'I've just had a great experience. Today I determined to see if I could do without my medicine. I had a terrible time – I couldn't sleep and had a lot of pain. Then I thought I heard God saying, "Mary, that was nothing to do with My will – you just determined!", so I took my medicine and had a lovely sleep'.

Then she looked at her son and said, 'That's what you need to learn: the difference between "I determined" and what God says .... '

~ LORNA LAIRD ~

ELIZABETH DOROTHY GARDNER

'GARDIE' —
the ZESTFUL DEACONESS

ELIZABETH DOROTHY GARDNER [1903–
1991] was the eldest daughter of a large
Edinburgh family. Although her first love
was dairy farming, she obeyed an irresist-
ible call to serve as a Church sister, the
fore-runner of the present-day deaconess.

After her training, she went to the
parishes of Lochgelly, Saltcoats, Stenhouse
(Edinburgh) and Greenock. Then in 1938
she moved to Cairns Memorial, Edinburgh
for 16 very rich and fruitful years. 'Gardie',
as she was affectionately known in the
community of Gorgie and beyond, was well
loved, especially by the children and young
people.

In 1954, aged 51, she began a new
career with the Church of Scotland Huts and
Canteens (first set up during World War II
to provide a social outlet for troops), serving
in Germany, then in Cyprus (during a war),
and later in Malaya.

From 1963–68, Gardie was President of
the Church of Scotland Deaconess Council,

hostess to and prime motivator of a memorable and historic Assembly of the World
Federation of Deaconess Associations held
in Edinburgh in 1966.

To the very end, new challenges beckon-
ed and excited Gardie and, much to her
delight, her last parish appointment took
her back to her early farming days at Thorn-
hill in Stirlingshire.

Retirement, first to Edinburgh and then
to Callander, freed Gardie for a life of prayer
and intercession for innumerable people.
She always had time for many causes and
concerns. Her faith was her life and she
found great joy in both. All the losses and
diminishments of her latter years were
faced with unconquerable grace, her bright
spirit and love of the Lord and his work
remaining as strong as ever.

Elizabeth Dorothy Gardner encompas-
sed within her long life an extraordinary and
rich variety of service, every phase of which
was marked with a blazingly infectious zest
and enthusiasm for life.

Jean Moncrieff, a young Sunday-school
teacher who was trained by Gardie, said
about this vital woman:

'Her faith shone, and it was through her
I first experienced the power of a telephone
prayer circle, when a young member of our
church was desperately ill. For over 45 years

I was able to call on Gardie for strength and support when my faith needed it. Her faith was her life and her joy. Her answer to every problem was – "I'll pray for you".

'She inspired me in so many ways and taught me that Faith works – I owe her a great debt.'

The last words belong to Gardie; she used them in her address to her deaconesses when she was their president: 'May you have much loving, learning and laughter'.

~ compiled by VIRGINIA WILKIE ~

GRANNY

A LESSON *in* TOLERANCE

I was only eight years old when my Granny died but she taught me an important lesson.

Granny was Roman Catholic. In our small town during the War, a priest was not always available to conduct Mass, so Granny came to the parish church with the rest of the family on those occasions.

From her, I had my first lesson in tolerance, respect for other people's beliefs and the importance of sharing the things which bind us together in worship, rather than dwelling on the differences that divide.

For she taught us that it is more important to worship regularly with other Christians than to worry about the form of that worship.

~ PEGGY MATTHEW ~

ELIZABETH HEWAT

HER *own* SECRET STAIR

ELIZABETH HEWAT was a very special
person – in many, many ways she was one
of the most outstanding women of her
generation. A daughter of the manse, she
was educated at Wellington School, Ayr,
and then at Edinburgh University and New
College, graduating with first class honours
in History and second class in Philosophy.
She was one of the first women to take the
degree of Bachelor of Divinity. Forty years
later she was to become the first woman
ever to be honoured by the university of
Edinburgh with the degree of Doctor of
Divinity.

With this quality of educational and
intellectual equipment, it was not surprising
that early on she favoured teaching, both
as an Assistant Lecturer in History at St
Andrews University and at St Colm's. She
then went to China where, for five years, she
combined her work as a teaching missionary
with so thorough a study of China and its
culture that she wrote her PhD thesis on 'A
comparison of Hebrew and Chinese Wisdom

as exemplified in the Book of Proverbs and the Analects of Confucius'.

After a brief break in 1933–34 she returned to the mission field and served in Wilson College, Bombay until retirement in 1956. Retirement for Elizabeth was anything but idle. She continued her writing – her contributions were already numerous to a variety of publications, from the *International Review of Missions*, to magazines for children like *Greatheart* and *Morning Rays*. Writing on their wavelength, she seemed to possess a remarkable talent for children's stories which was revealed in her early days, but which found full expression in her last years.

She also wrote many thoughtful and inspiring, yet basically simple, Bible study books, revealing the quality of her mind, the depth of her devotion, the strength of her faith and the warmth of her understanding.

During her period as a National Vice-President of the Woman's Guild, Elizabeth toured the country tirelessly, giving of herself, even though her own health was failing. She was especially remembered for her humility – while she espoused with vehemence causes like the Campaign for Nuclear Disarmament (CND) and Women in the Ministry, she always understood and made allowances for those who differed from her.

However, she never allowed her fine mind to be narrowed down in any direction – that mind was open to a great variety of ideas and causes. But even more distinctive was the breadth and warmth of her interest in people.

Elizabeth is also remembered for that saving grace – her sense of humour. Beneath a sometimes forbidding exterior, not helped by ever-increasing deafness, she could never conceal a sense of fun and friendliness, of her sheer delight in living which enriched all who knew her.

At the heart of it all, the long life of varied achievement in China, India and Scotland, the miles travelled, the millions of words written or spoken in many languages, the warmth of caring for so many of 'all manner of folk' – the true explanation of this rare life was that Elizabeth Hewat had her own secret stair to the near presence of the Master, whose she was and whom she sought to serve.

[*Based upon material provided by Leonard Small.*]

JEAN
MARY
FRASER

Under the CROSS

JEAN FRASER took up office as Principal of St Colm's College, Edinburgh in September of 1955. At the same time I entered the College, a very raw, unfledged Christian, coming from the world of newspaper reporting, understanding nothing about the nature of the Church, except for a clear conviction that the Lord wanted me to serve there. I was really in the dark – but not for long.

Like a resounding trumpet call, Jean opened the shutters of my understanding and let in floods of light. From being a solitary Christian with no congregational roots, I discovered through Jean and her marvellous team of colleagues (Effie Gray, Frank Ryrie and Janet Watson) the nature of Christian community, the Communion of Saints, the world-wide Church. I had encountered the truth that Jean lived by – 'the totality of the Church in the whole world, embracing the totality of life'.

JEAN
MARY
FRASER

Jean's own life made it plain that every interest and aptitude could be taken up into the Lord's service, renewed and put to use.

As a born leader, she was involved from childhood in Christian youth groups. At Cambridge, studying modern languages, she was immersed also in the Student Christian Movement and in issues of social justice.

Commissioned as Church Sister in the Presbyterian Church of England, she was appointed to Stepney, where she was part of an extraordinary team, working with joy and commitment among the people of the docklands. During the Blitz of World War II, Jean was right there by their sides, through 89 nights of continuous bombing.

In 1939 when the first World Conference of Christian Youth was held in Amsterdam, Jean played a key role. The young people, gathered in Amsterdam just before the out-break of the War, experienced an event deeply charged with emotion yet irradiated with hope.

In 1942, Jean became Secretary of the British Council of Churches and in 1947 she went to Geneva to a similar post in the newly formed World Council of Churches.

The story of Jean Mary Fraser was one of a dynamic personality and a powerful mind with, at the heart's core, unbelievable simplicity and humility.

Jean gave me and countless others what I needed most – the assurance of friendship with boundless understanding and warmth, directed always to companionship on the spiritual journey, 'under the Cross'.

Under the Cross was the title of a book she wrote in 1955. She wrote of the Church sharing, to the point of suffering and sacrifice, Christ's outgoing love to all the world, and of dying to all self-concern.

Jean's own journey has been increasingly 'under the Cross', yet through all this, every thought of her must be one of thanksgiving and praise to her Lord.

~ KAY RAMSAY ~

JANET

Live LIFE *to the* FULL

The 8th of September 1992 was a very
special day for **JANET** – her 90th birthday.
It was a day to be enjoyed, from the arrival
of the postman weighed down with greet-
ings cards and presents, to the excitement
of putting on a brand new dress in fashionable purple, ready to be taken out by the
family for dinner at a local hotel.

Two younger sisters, one from London,
the other from the Isle of Man, had made
the trip to be with her on this memorable
occasion. Janet was surrounded by people
she loved and cared for. She was happy.

It was not always so – her life had indeed
been 'hard', coming into the world at the
beginning of the twentieth century when
parents strived long hours to provide enough
food and clothing for large families. Janet
was born in Avoch, a small fishing village
on the Black Isle. She was baptised in her
cradle when only a day old – she was so ill it
was thought she would not see the day out.

Her parents were fisherfolk and devoted
members of the local Congregational

Church. The whole family attended Church twice every Sunday, the children going with their father to Sunday School in the afternoon. In the evening there was singing and fellowship in neighbouring homes.

Tragedy struck, however. When Janet was barely 14 her mother died and shortly afterwards her father was drowned in a freak accident. The family was orphaned. An aunt offered to care for one of the girls, and two other children were sent to an orphanage. Janet brought up and cared for the other four.

Six years later, now 21, Janet took over the care of another family – she married a widower with five daughters. As if that were not enough, her husband was a farm manager and this meant that his wife had to cook and care for two or three unmarried farm workers in addition to her growing family. Janet later had four of her own children – two boys and two girls.

Life was certainly all go, but not in the way we term a full life today – 13 children to care for, plus an additional niece from London evacuated for a few months during World War II, and a nephew who was left motherless from the age of eight.

Janet retired from work at the age of 70, when she gave up her job helping in the local primary school canteen.

She sits back now, with time to reflect over the years. She talks of her Church, her 69 years of commitment to her local Church of Scotland congregation in Knockbain. She speaks of her delight in the gift of a large-print copy of the Gospels and Psalms given to her by her grandson and his wife – a gift which has not been re-wrapped and put away, but is taken out two or three times every day and read.

She does however have one sorrow – she missed the last communion service in the Church. For the first time she had not been able to attend the service which has given her strength and sustained her throughout 34 years of married life and 35 years of widowhood. And why did she miss her favourite service? It was not because of her difficulty in making out the words in the hymn book, not because she can only hear some of the words spoken, nor because she would not be able to manage the steps down from the Church (because doesn't the minister always help her?) – no, it was because her hands now shake so badly she was afraid of dropping the bread and spilling the wine.

Strangely, though, Janet does not speak of her faith. But *is* that strange for a woman who was born into faith, who survived by faith, who was brought up by faith and who lived by faith; for someone who knew that her very breath was a gift from God and that every day of her life was given to her through His grace. Her faith is so integral to her life, so woven into the warp and woof of all the events of the last 90 years that it cannot be extricated, it cannot be separated and put to one side and labelled 'faith'.

For Janet, life is only lived by faith and to have faith in this life is to live life to the full, fully committed to walk in His way to His glory and honour, sustained only by His love.

~ RUTH CAMPBELL-JACK ~

The
GIFT *of*
SERENITY

FAITH *in* GOD

In my early teenage schooldays, I remember
a teacher who said to us, 'If you girls are
not beautiful in your old age, it's your own
fault. Beauty comes from character, not
cosmetics'.

This was made real for me by a member
of my Guild branch when I was President.
She was an elderly lady who always sat in
the front row, always keen and attentive,
and she had a serene and lovely face. Yet I
knew how hard her life had been in the
past – her husband was a drunken, brutal
man. When he came home, the worse for
drink, she had to escape into the backgreen
to hide. Although she never complained,
the neighbours knew what was happening.

From this old friend I learned that faith
in God can bring deliverance from self-pity
and bitterness, which can so easily harden
the heart and crush the spirit. She certainly
turned me Godwards.

~ LORNA LAIRD ~

GLIMPSES
of HOPE
from AFRICA

ABITIMO — *building a* SCHOOL

In 1991 in Caux, Switzerland, at an international conference on 'Creators of Peace' initiated by women of Africa, I met ABITIMO, a lady from Uganda, who told me her story.

She had nurtured a vision of starting a school in her village, but during the repressive government of Idi Amin, she was forced to flee to America. While there, somebody paid for her to be trained as a teacher.

When she returned to Uganda, she and her friends bought a plot of land and built a school with their own hands. She was hoping to expand but civil war broke out, and they all had to flee to the town.

In the town Abitimo watched children playing in the street with nothing to do, nowhere to go. She took a dozen or so of them under a tree and began to teach. Bit by bit the numbers grew until there were hundreds of eager pupils. Abitimo had achieved her school — she had a vision, she enlisted the help of others, and her faith in God gave her the strength to carry that vision through.

BARBARA —
training MIDWIVES

While working in a mission college in the south-east of Nigeria, I became friendly with a midwifery tutor – BARBARA – who had come to Africa as a missionary all the way from Holland. This was in the late '70s, after a horrific civil war, when the poverty, dejection and lack of infra-structure were evident all around.

Barbara's task was to train girls to be midwives. There was a hospital in the township with lots of patients, but nothing else – no building for training, no equipment, no accommodation. It would be hard enough for a lone woman to build such an institution in her own country, but it would be nothing in comparison to Nigeria, where every negotiation meant lonely and hazardous car journeys over impassable roads to Lagos over 400 miles away – often only to be met with further frustrations. Even trips to her own state capital would involve endless wrangling and cajoling.

Fortunately, the village people rallied round and eventually, with their help and with equipment from Holland, they built the whole compound – a credit to the folk of the area.

Girls with very little primary education were now able to be trained into first class midwives, becoming an asset to their area and to their country.

Barbara believed that she had been sent to do a job and she never lost the vision of what that midwifery school should be. She had faith in God and in the friends she had made to continue until her task had been completed.

PEGGY — *encouraging* FRIENDSHIPS

Years ago, when I worked in a Manchester hospital, I was friendly with a nurse called **PEGGY** who worked in a nearby Ear Hospital. When her younger sister, Mary, became ill, Peggy gave up her hospital job to care for her.

Peggy and Mary together helped Mary's husband to find his faith and the three worked as a team, praying together and sharing much happiness with each other.

Sadly Mary died in 1950. Peggy decided at that time to visit another sister in Zimbabwe. Once there, she found that she loved Africa and a persistent thought began to whisper to her that she should stay on in Africa. This was about the time of the

unilateral declaration of independence of
Rhodesia, and Peggy saw herself working
to bring people together in that unsettled
country. So she took a job as a nurse in a
tin-making factory in Bulawayo, making
friends with the factory workers and many
other folk in the town and beyond.

When Peggy retired, she bought a flat
bigger than she needed in Harare, so that
people of all colours and persuasions would
have a home where they could talk out their
differences and learn to understand each
other. That home became a valuable contribution to the relatively smooth change from
Rhodesia to Zimbabwe.

When Peggy died, her home was given
over to continue the work of reconciliation,
where the standards of Jesus Christ –
honesty, purity, unselfishness and love –
are badly needed. Peggy, inspired by a sick
sister, learned to stand alone and found a
vision for her adopted country.

~ RUTH KNOX ~

FAITHFUL
PRAYER

waiting on the LORD

Sadly it is often the case that, only when
they have gone from us, do we become
aware of the volume of prayer work done
on our behalf by our Christian parents. I
certainly found this to be the case.

Mother introduced my brothers and myself to prayer in the very early stages of our
lives. My first recollection was at the age of
three, kneeling with my brothers, as my
mother guided us through our stumbling
prayers. She affirmed in our young lives the
need for us to talk with God before we
slept, reminding us of his protecting love.
I'm sure this dispelled much of the childish
fear of darkness if we awoke in the night.

At breakfast, a book of prayers by Bishop
Bickersteth was always at my mother's
place and from this she read each morning.
One phrase stays in my mind: 'Go before us
today, O Lord, as the breaker up of our path-
way'. I had a vision of God clearing the
rocks and boulders strewn on life's road, and
the thought that He was out there was a
happy reassurance.

From the faith which exuded from my mother's prayer life, I grew to feel that God was always near me. But I had yet to learn so much, not least respect and reverence for my God. On one occasion, with the audacity of a child, I thought to put God to the test.

Much to my shame, this was for purely selfish reasons. My parents had entertained some friends to dinner. After the meal, mother suggested that I start to clear the table – well, I was quickly on my knees asking God to undertake this work for me! Then I'd know he was my friend and that he *did* answer prayers. Such an opportunity for God!

As you can imagine, when I arose from bargaining with God, the state of the table had not changed and with considerable disappointment I set to work.

Later I spoke to my mother, saying that I was a bit puzzled over God's reluctance to help me out with a small miracle. She asked me whether I would ask my best friend to do all my work whilst I sat back and watched, just to *prove* she was my best friend. That got the point home and it has stayed in my heart for ever.

My mother was always keen that children should learn reverence, but also *enjoy* prayer, particularly in infancy. I've heard her say to her friends, 'Pray without ceasing for your children, but oh! – do pray *with* them'.

She also spoke of 'waiting on the Lord in prayer'. I asked her once whether she ever worried about her children not becoming Christians. 'Indeed,' she replied, 'but my strength lay in the fact that I prayed you all into The Kingdom before you were born.'

Later on, I found that my busy days squeezed out much of my prayer life and I tended to rush at God when a crisis arose. I was unaware of how sterile my daily devotions had become. One day, chatting to my mother about the church we were then attending in Glasgow, she asked me if we were going to attend the prayer meeting there – and she made it clear that this was not optional. That prayer meeting was to become a sanctuary for us as a family.

My nephew, on leaving the house one morning at dawn, heard mother praying – naming each member of her family before God. 'She spoke as if He was sitting at her bedside,' he said, 'but with such reverence.'

I discovered that, in our household and in the homes of my brothers, my mother's influence took root and we all started our day with prayers, including the children when they were still very young. It became obvious, as time wore on, that our young folk found great security in prayer – noticeably so on examination days. Guess who were first in the 'Prayer Circle' on those days!

Mother prayed especially for 'the Church in our dear land of Scotland'. Many of the ministers she had never met, but she looked forward to meeting them one day 'when we all go home'.

Each morning she brought our Royal Family, the Prime Minister, and members of Parliament to God in prayer. I recall that Mr Gorbachev, when he was head of USSR, was also frequently brought to the throne of grace. Sometimes I wonder whether it was the faithful prayers of such women as my mother, in this and other lands, which were instrumental in bringing about the new freedom now enjoyed by Christians in Eastern Europe.

My mother believed with St Paul that 'by means of God's power in us, He is able to do much more than we can ever ask for'. Her life has proved to me that it is through faithful and quiet prayer that God moves mountains.

~ MARGARET LAING ~

GRANNY
CLARK

Radiating FAITH

'What! 278!?' a friend of **GRANNY CLARK** exclaimed. No, it was not the number of people at the last Guild Presbyterial Rally, nor was it the number of people in Church last Sunday. 278 is the actual number of people on Granny Clark's prayer list.

How? Simple – every time friends ask her to pray for a relative or friend, their name goes on the list. If they are ill or really in need of prayer for something, she prays for them by name and gives the reason for bringing them to the throne of grace. When the real need for prayer is past, Granny Clark continues to name them. No names are crossed off the list until death. Granny Clark certainly believes in answered prayer.

What a feat! What a faith she must have to enable such a tremendous undertaking! So, what in her life has made her the woman of faith she now is?

Let's start at the beginning of her story. Not unusually for someone of her generation, Granny Clark was born and baptised into a Christian family, attended Sunday

School and was confirmed. Although she lived in London, she married a Scotsman and soon after the wedding came to live in Kirkcaldy. From there she moved to Edinburgh, then to Inverness and back again to Edinburgh. In each place she became a member of the parish Church of Scotland, joined the choir and became an active committee member of the Woman's Guild.

In October 1965, when she was 59, an American evangelistic group came to the Usher Hall in Edinburgh. She joined the 300 strong supporting choir, thrilled to be participating in the mass musical. She decided to enjoy the singing and ignore the preaching. But Granny Clark little realised that this event was going to prove a watershed in her life.

One particular night, the speaker's voice just seemed to grip her. As she stood up to sing the last hymn – 'Just as I am, without one plea, but that Thy blood was shed for me' – it seemed that she did indeed know Jesus Christ as her Saviour and felt the inflowing gift of His Holy Spirit.

From that day on, Granny Clark lived her life to God's glory – in greater depth, with a new dimension and outlook. Worship was no longer a formality, a duty, or a habit. It came alive – as her life took on more purpose and meaning. This life is only a journey; one day Granny Clark will go on to greater and better things, to life eternal.

But what of the here and now? At the moment Granny Clark is a member of St Davids Broomhouse Church in Edinburgh. She has worshipped there for 35 years, since the good old days when the church itself was merely two army huts. (It was back in those days that the young folk gave her the endearing name 'Granny Clark'.) For many years she was a regular at the mid-week prayer meeting and she still continues to attend church twice on Sunday.

As she looks back over her life recounting tales and telling stories, her sense of humour breaks through time and time again. Her constant chuckle indicates a love for the life which she knows is God's gift to her by His grace. She is indeed one of those rare breed of Christians who not only live by faith, but who *radiate* it – a witness to all.

~ Ruth Campbell-Jack ~

LILY
WALKER

The THINGS *of the* SPIRIT

When in 1956 the Walkers moved in next door to us, I thought at first that they were the grandparents of the young boy of two who came with them. I later discovered that they were the child's parents.

LILY WALKER was born and brought up in Glasgow, nurtured in the Christian faith. She worked at the Co-op shop there, but the urge for Christian service was so strong within her that she applied for missionary work overseas. This was refused by the powers-that-be, but she was offered instead the opportunity to train at St Colm's to become a deaconess. In this capacity she served in Shotts for many years.

When her sister died, Lily felt concern and compassion for her brother-in-law, and later married him. I think she would have liked to carry on her work as deaconess, which she loved, but after a year, now 48, she presented her husband with a son, much to his great delight. He had become a father for the first time at the age of 60.

My first feelings towards Lily Walker

were, strangely, of resentment – she quickly became absorbed into all the local church activities and I felt she should have concentrated more on the upbringing of her son. I can see now that I was wrong – Lily had so much to offer to *all* of us.

Although we clashed at first, we soon developed a mutual respect for one another, until, gradually, we struck up a great friendship. I have to say, Lily was as sharp as a serpent and not always as harmless as a dove – she could lash out when angry. I can still remember some of her quick retorts:

'I come from Yorkshire,' I said to her once, rather smugly, after a bit of a set-to. 'We speak our minds there.'

'Ah,' came the shrewd reply, 'funny how people who pride themselves on speaking their minds can never take it when others do it to them!'

True, very true!

On another occasion, I said to her, 'I like best being with people who are intellectually or spiritually my superior'.

'Well, that's a very selfish attitude,' she responded. 'You just want to receive rather than give of yourself.'

I'd never thought of it that way!

Every second Friday, Lily and I used to visit each other's house, turn about, at about 9 o'clock for a light supper. Then we would talk and talk into the wee sma' hours on the things of the Spirit. Different aspects of theology were given an airing and often argued over, but sometimes whole new truths were revealed to both of us and we felt that God was in there somewhere with us.

Lily was a very outgoing person, full of warmth and compassion, whereas I had been a more private individual as far as my faith was concerned. Whenever someone was in trouble, she would go immediately to their house.

'Won't that be a bit of an intrusion?' I would say to her, 'I'd want to be alone with my grief.'

But, seeing the outcomes, how wrong I was again!

Last year, when I lost my husband, I learned how much I appreciated the love and support I received from so many people. No way would I have wanted to be alone with my grief – just one example of how her faith had influenced and matured my own Christian thinking.

Yes, I learned a lot from Lily Walker and I owe her a great debt.

~ GWEN CLARK ~

JOY
IRVINE

The POWER *of* PRAYER

I have never forgotten that extraordinary, unforgettable moment! It occurred around 1970, when my husband and I were working with Mission Aviation Fellowship, based in up-country Ethiopia. That year, I had travelled south to Kenya, to enjoy a brief holiday in the capital, Nairobi.

One morning a stranger tapped on the door, walked straight in and, to my utter astonishment, enclosed me in a long, warm embrace. Then she stood back and exclaimed, 'Elaine, it's so good to see you! I praise God that we've met at last! You see, through prayer I've really grown to love you'.

I was amazed. Who was this smiling, warm-hearted stranger? How did she know me so well? I was soon to discover – and it was the start of one of the most rich and valued friendships I have known.

The stranger was **Mrs JOY IRVINE**, wife of the much respected Dr Clive who, years earlier, had started the important Church of Scotland medical ministry at Chogoria. By the time I met Joy, she and Clive had retired to Nairobi where Joy gave herself to a whole new ministry – the ministry of prayer.

With her mind focussed on the demands of our flying work and busy home, Joy gave herself to imaginative, eager prayer on our behalf. How many potential flying hazards was my pilot husband spared? How often did my own strength to cope come as a direct result of Joy's prayer-care? I will never know.

One thing I do know, Joy prayed with such fervent involvement that she became ONE with us as a family, and also with the many others for whom she cared in this way. Each belonged to her, and was prayerfully cherished by her.

Over the few remaining years, before Joy died, we corresponded regularly and the bond deepened. I have kept her letters. I have also kept and treasured the remarkable prayer example she set. Unknowingly, Joy opened up a whole new aspect of prayer for me. She taught me that in praying for a person, you grow increasingly to love them – this fills prayer with powerful potential. It's exciting! I have begun to discover this for myself, but I have still a long way to go.

When asked to name a person who has inspired my faith, my immediate thought is of Joy. The Lord continues to enrich me through her.

~ ELAINE BROWN ~

MARTHA

An INFECTIOUS FAITH

I first met **MARTHA** during the Blitz when my office was evacuated from London to Wales. A few days after my arrival in Llandudno, she called at my billet and invited me to coffee, explaining that a mutual friend had given her my address.

During my last months in London, I had tried to ignore an uneasy feeling that a course of action, on which I had set my heart, might not be God's plan for me. In fact I had found it more comfortable of late to avoid certain friends who might challenge me to find out if I really was doing the right thing – so, naturally, I was wary of Martha.

That first evening, however, led to others and we became friends. Her honesty and her faith were infectious and soon I decided that I too needed to find out exactly what God wanted me to do with my life. This meant taking time to listen to Him – somewhat awkward in an over-crowded billet! My room-mate objected, perhaps not unreasonably, to being wakened at an unearthly hour, when I put on the single light in our attic bedroom to read my Bible and write down the thoughts that came to me as I tried to seek guidance.

Martha, who lived quite near the billet, came to the rescue by inviting me to join her in the morning when we could pray and listen to God together. For several mornings a week, I crept down the attic stair and walked through the blacked-out streets to her home, to be welcomed with a cup of tea.

Martha's ambition from an early age, she told me, had been to serve in a shop. She started as a message girl in a fashionable shop in the days when ladies had their hats and dresses delivered to their homes in large cardboard boxes. By the time I met her, she was buyer in a large department store. During the War, when all clothes were 'on coupons', this was sometimes a difficult job. It was tempting to think that there were circumstances in which bending the rules was justified, but Martha knew that, with wartime shortages, rationing was necessary if available goods were to be distributed fairly. She was certainly not prepared to 'oblige' customers by turning a blind eye to dishonest practices. Customers informed her that other shops were 'more helpful', and took their custom elsewhere. Others, however, appreciated her policy of honesty – some even began to have second thoughts about the morality of the black market. Many customers were to become Martha's friends. Knowing that she could be trusted, some brought their problems to her.

For Martha, serving customers meant giving them the best she could. Even within the limitations of rationing and shortages, she thought there was no excuse for women to be dowdy. On one occasion I took a fancy to a most unsuitable dress, so I tried it on. Martha took one look at me, swept it over my head and put it back on the rail.

'I wouldn't sell it to you,' she said.

No doubt she was more tactful with customers she did not know so well, but to her it was more important for customers to have what was right for them, than to make a sale.

Now in her 80s, Martha continues to share her faith with friends and neighbours and still welcomes visitors to her home, as she welcomed me.

~ ANON ~

The DEER

A PARABLE *of* LIFE

On her bedside cabinet, shortly after my mother's death, I found a newspaper cutting. It brought me much comfort at a time of sorrow and loss. This is the gist of the story.

A keen photographer hid one winter's night in the attic of an old cottage in Glen Clunie, hoping to catch sight of a herd of deer. It was very cold, with showers of sleet whipped up by an arctic wind. The man was numb, but no deer appeared and he left the cottage disappointed.

The next evening, just beyond Braemar, a large herd suddenly came into view. There were so many animals that the photographer was almost tumbling over them. He and a companion counted them – 147 in total, quietly grazing near the River Dee.

Then, in the late gloaming, the men were thrilled to see a small group of deer splash through the shallow water of the river and swim the main channel to the north bank, where they remained, motionless.

At the same time another herd was gathering in the dusk on the south side of the river. They stood in the water as if afraid to cross. The photographer watched, hardly daring to breathe, as a stag detached himself from the group on the north bank, plunged into the water and swam right up to where the faint-hearts stood. He made an about-turn into the deep water again – now closely followed by all the faltering animals. Soon every creature was safely across the river.

To the photographer and his companion, it seemed as if the stag had whispered to the frightened animals, 'Come on – don't be frightened. I've been here myself, there's nothing to fear. Just follow me and I will lead you safely across'.

Those men beheld a true parable of life that night. Most of us face difficulties on life's road, where doubt and fear bring us to a halt. The very last mile of the way, described by the Psalmist as 'the valley of the shadow of death', is such a halting place.

These words have always been very significant to me – 'Just follow me and I will lead you safely across'. Was that my mother's way of saying to me she was not afraid to die?

~ PRISCILLA MCLEOD ~

The FAITH *of* YOUTH *and* AGE

SARAH *and* PETER

In 1975 a young couple – SARAH and PETER – came over from Scotland to an African bush hospital shortly after a tragic civil war.

Everyone there was depressed. The hospital had deteriorated through lack of funds, manpower and will-power. The only trained staff were the matron and chief nursing officer and all the nurses were educated to an average level of primary 3.

All three wards were overcrowded – one for maternity, one for males, one for females and children. Even more neglected was an annexe for tuberculosis and leprosy patients. An ex-patriot doctor visited twice a week.

The hospital served a wide area, catering for a quarter of a million people. The only transport was the hospital land rover. Even in that, it could take an hour and a half to reach the main road. Often a bridge was down and during the rainy season even the toughest vehicle could get stuck in mud. For a month soon after the couple arrived, they could not communicate with the outside world even for food and petrol. Telephones were unheard of. They had a water tank to collect rain and an electric generator which often broke down, meaning that operations had to be carried out by torchlight. There was not enough power to use an electric iron or kettle, and food was stored and prepared in a kerosene fridge and cooker.

Peter, who had to practise as physician, surgeon *and* gynaecologist, worked all his waking hours. His wife Sarah, who trained as a nurse in the UK, was not allowed to begin work until she was granted a work permit, which took months to come. So she spent the time cleaning and painting their home which was in a deplorable state.

Once the work permit came through, Sarah worked voluntarily, but ceaselessly, training the nurses to carry out their jobs efficiently, despite educational limitations. She also helped to teach the mothers basic nutrition and hygiene. Despite numerous frustrations and set-backs, the family atmosphere of faith and eagerness to help was obvious throughout the hospital. Sarah entered wholeheartedly into the work of the nearby church, Woman's Guild and all the local celebrations. In time, her own children were all born in the hospital.

Before Sarah left in 1981, her cherished dream of having a children's ward in the bush hospital came true.

HILDA

An elderly couple moved house to enjoy retirement together in a comfortable flat near their son. Barely three weeks later, the husband died of a sudden heart attack. All his wife's dreams of a happy retirement were shattered. If it had not been for her faith, she would have gone under – but HILDA had been used to seeking God's will for each day and studying his word. This helped her through that early painful time.

She soon began to become aware of the people around her and she took to inviting students into her new home. Like Hilda, they too were away from familiar home and friends. She also made friends with her immediate neighbours, especially those in a nearby student flat, taking such an interest in them that they felt at ease with her.

She also put her culinary skills to good use, helping her son and daughter-in-law entertain their many friends and colleagues. Anyone entering either home, expected or unannounced, immediately experienced the warm atmosphere.

Soon Hilda made friends with the people in her church. Being a downtown church, many students attended and she enjoyed befriending these young people.

Hilda has faith that God works in many different ways, so not only does she live what she believes, but she also keeps an attractive display of books in her lobby full of the life stories and reminiscences of like-minded folk. Visitors are welcome to browse. And, although well over 80, Hilda has a video cassette player and knows how to work it. So she is well able to show *all* her friends what she has learned from other people, watching fascinating stories – full of humour, humility and inspiration.

Nothing daunts Hilda. If she believes something is right, she will go through with it, at whatever cost – a book fair in a church hall or her own home; an elaborate meal for an honoured visitor; a bed for the night; soup and a sandwich for an unexpected guest. Nothing is too much trouble.

Not long ago, Hilda attended a conference in India where she had stayed years before with her husband. She took the young girls she met there to her heart and has kept up correspondence with them ever since, encouraging them in their desire to find God's will for their lives.

Hilda continues to encourage young people and to inspire other octogenarians to live each day to the full, however limited their physical health and mobility.

~ RUTH KNOX ~

CATHERINE HUNTER

WOMAN *of* FAITH

Mothers are greatly loved. So it was with my mother. She was a very special lady to many people. Her name was CATHERINE HUNTER – 'Cath' to all her friends.

Born in Spittalfield, Perthshire in the late nineteenth century, Cath was one of a family of seven. Her childhood was shadowed by disability – namely a short left leg. This rendered her unable to keep up with the other children. Suggestion of an operation was rejected by her mother who felt the risk was too great – she stated simply that God would look after her daughter. So the decision was made, and she managed to disguise her noticeably short left leg fairly successfully all through her life.

Cath's faith was so great that no problems were too much to bear. She would simply smile and carry on in her own delightful way. She went on to marry and have children, but, in 1939, tragedy struck – she lost her only son after a short illness. He was eighteen years old.

After months of grief for her and the

family, World War II began. Cath was grateful to God that she had been spared the trauma of seeing her son off to war. She at least had been able to be with him during his illness, and had not lost him on a foreign battlefield.

With renewed vigour, Cath threw herself into activity aimed at helping other people. She worked in the local canteen for Polish soldiers billeted in the town, the soldiers falling under her spell, as she mastered the Polish words for 'thank you' and 'matches'. She cared for them all and made them feel welcome in a strange country. To them she was like a mother.

The Woman's Guild of St Andrew's Church, Coupar Angus, was her other great interest. She was Tea Convener for many years.

During the War, two daughters left home to follow nursing careers, so Cath was left with an ailing husband to care for. Not forgetting her, the daughters saved their meagre sugar ration for many weeks and took it home for Cath to use. One of the girls went to Jerusalem with the Queen Alexandra's Nursing Service, and she despatched home a supply of currants and raisins. They were promptly used for the Woman's Guild teas. Everything Cath ever had, she shared.

She also helped and encouraged everyone with whom she came in contact. As her grandchildren grew up, she played her part with loving care – they loved her very much.

The theme in Cath's life was that God would provide. When, in later years, her eyesight grew dim, latterly non-existent, she continued to lead a very useful life, fully confident she would be looked after. She was indeed a woman of faith.

~ MABEL RICHARDS ~

SAIDIE PATTERSON

The BRIDGE-BUILDER

SAIDIE PATTERSON was born into a
Protestant working class family in Belfast.
From the beginning she knew hardship,
but her caring mother always said, 'If you
see something wrong and do nothing about
it to put it right, you are part of the wrong'.

This was a lesson she never forgot, and
when sectarian violence broke out in
Northern Ireland, she set to work to bridge
the gap between Catholics and Protestants.

Saidie became chairperson of an
organisation called Women Together, and
helped to organise a march of thousands of
women along the Shanklin Road.

'Today,' she said to the women, 'we
marched not as Catholics or Protestants,
but as children of the King of Kings.'

When I first met her in a friend's house
in Edinburgh in 1980, she told us how she
made a note of all the families, Protestant
and Catholic, who had lost a father through
the strife. She visited each of these families
and did what she could to comfort them.

At that time, I was giving house room

to three dressed dolls which had been left on the stall at a recent Guild Sale of Work. Inspired by Saidie's example, I decided to buy the dolls myself and send them to Saidie for the children of some of those families. At the next Guild meeting, I asked if I could do this in the name of Priestfield Church Guild. The Guild members agreed and some of them said they would like to add other toys. Another member offered to pay the postage for what now had become a rather large parcel.

After Christmas, Saidie wrote to say that she had delivered the gifts to bereaved families on Christmas morning – not from Santa Claus, but from a Scottish Protestant Woman's Guild. One of the mothers said, with tears in her eyes, 'Now I believe that other people do really care'.

Saidie received many awards for her work for peace and reconciliation. As well as the MBE, presented to her by the Queen, she was given the World Methodist Peace award, and became the first Irish woman to receive an Open University honorary degree.

Saidie was essentially a bridge-builder, working ceaselessly to close the gulf between Protestant and Catholics.

Sadly she died a few years ago.

~ JEAN McNEILL ~

MARY
DALGLEISH

The ENCOURAGER

MARY DALGLEISH was born in Bournemouth
in 1922 and brought up in the Church of
England, although her family background
was Wesleyan. After school, she trained as a
nurse, became ward sister and then quali-
fied as a midwife. She met her husband Neil
in 1943. They married in 1947 and moved
to his home in Edinburgh. There she became
a member of the Church of Scotland, becoming involved with the Young Wives and
Mothers Group – the start of a life-long
commitment to the Woman's Guild.

Mary spoke lovingly of her Guild friendships, both in Edinburgh and the Borders –
her 'chums', as she called them. She valued
such friendships and went out of her way to
keep in touch. She was happy to help out in
any way – stewarding at Usher Hall Guild
meetings or standing in for a sick secretary.

Lena Lees writes about Mary: 'I met her
when I joined the Business Committee of
Edinburgh South Presbyterial Council, and
she was secretary during my first year as
president. It was quite some time before I

learned that she suffered from the severe medical handicap of asthma. She *never* talked about it, and this, to me, was a measure of her faith – the courage with which she managed to live such a full, busy, worthwhile life, serving the Master in whom she believed so completely ... We attended a number of retreats together, taking part in many Bible study sessions, where Mary's contributions were wise and thought-provoking and always came from the heart'.

In 1972, the Dalgleishes moved to Bowden, near Melrose, where Mary became involved in church and community with the same enthusiasm and commitment. Grace Hutchison, the parish minister's wife, became a close friend of Mary's, and served with her in the local branch of the Guild.

Grace recalls: 'Mary was a lady of many gifts and talents – always expressing an intelligent and balanced opinion on important matters – always revealing the strength of her personal faith ... Her great love was for her husband, Neil, and their family. They regularly visited their three children, all abroad, and so kept family ties strong. Every time they visited us, they produced photographs of their grandchildren who meant so much to them.'

In the community, Mary was interested in all things and all people. She worked for

the Central Borders Citizens Advice Bureau,
as an adviser and on the management committee. Colleagues remember her wisdom
and commitment to her work and the
training involved. She was always a great
'encourager', playing a full part but content
to remain in the background.

In 1978 Mary Dalgleish was appointed
a Justice of the Peace for Ettrick and Lauder-
dale District. Seven years later she was given
the CBE for her community work. This work
included an interest in politics. For many
years she served the Conservative Party at
Association level in Edinburgh and the
Borders, eventually becoming Vice-President of the Conservative Party in Scotland.

For four years until 1982, Mary was a
member of the Kirk's Church and Nation
Committee. She served loyally on Melrose
Presbyterial Council and her strong faith,
her commitment, her graciousness, are all
well-remembered. Not one to seek the lime-
light, she encouraged others into becoming
involved, giving practical help – a book
here, a prayer there – and a listening ear.
Few people knew of her health problems.

Mary's sudden death in 1991 brought
sadness to many. 'Mary had so much still to
give,' Grace Hutchison said, 'but not many
have so much to show for their lifetime.'

~ *compiled by* MARJORIE LAWRIE ~

IRINA
RATUSHINSKAYA

IRINA RATUSHINSKAYA is a Russian poet
who, on her 29th birthday, was sentenced
to seven years in a Soviet labour camp, to
be followed by five years internal exile. Her
'crime' was her poetry.

At university her poems, reflecting her
Christian faith and integrity, brought her
to the attention of the KGB which led to
her trial and imprisonment. Four years later
she was released after intensive campaign-
ing in the West.

She is now resident with her husband
and children in the United Kingdom, and I
heard her speak and answer questions in an
East Lothian school, where she autographed
a copy of her book for me – *Grey is the Colour
of Hope* – about her prison experiences.

She talked to the young people at the
school about hatred – how Christ forbade
it, how in a prison camp you could be
destroyed by hatred because everything is
designed to make you hate.

'If you start to hate, you can never stop,'
she said. 'To hold on to your personality, to

survive, even to keep your common sense, you have to kill hatred immediately. Then you understand Christ's words about hatred. And, of course, those who know how to get rid of it can help others better.'

Of the guards who treated them so harshly, she said, 'You could only pity them'.

Irina was also asked how it is that people who have suffered often have so much to give.

She said, 'When people suffer, as we really had to suffer, they sometimes get a better understanding of how Christ can help them in everyday life .... Suffering itself is neutral. It can break people down and destroy them, or it can make them stronger. One thing I have noticed – it is not the suffering itself which breaks people down, it is the *fear* of suffering. People in the West can be equally afraid – of nuclear war, or the greenhouse effect, or inflation. It is the constant fear of some probable future suffering which can break you down – or it can make you stronger with equal success if you face it'.

Hatred and suffering – both so prevalent in the world today. Here was an answer to them from a woman of faith who had experienced so much.

~ LORNA LAIRD ~

MOYRA
STEWART

My GOD *is* REAL

There comes a time of realisation for some people that God is real and that He loves us. For **MOYRA STEWART**, this happened over a period of years. She was not brought up in a church-going family, and only began to think about religion during her nursing career, her faith in God strengthened bit by bit. During particular crises, she came to know God and to realise that she was special to Him and that He loved her. As she read in Romans: 'Now that we have been put right with God through faith, we have peace with God through our Lord Jesus Christ' (Romans 5:1, GNB).

Moyra was to have her faith in God, and the peace and joy she had found, severely challenged by an event which nearly cost her her life. Moyra assisted her husband in the preparation of prize bulls for show and sale at local agricultural auction markets. One day, during October 1990, she was grooming the bulls, each weighing over a ton, when one of them kicked over the pail she was using. This startled both bulls and

they began to lash out. Moyra was kicked
to the ground and remembers curling up to
try to save her face. She remained conscious
throughout, but, strangely enough, did not
feel frightened. She thought only about
how to position herself for protection and
prayed: 'Lord, I am not ready to die, but if
You want me, I am willing to go'.

Moyra was not expected to survive and
spent the next six weeks undergoing several
operations. But, despite many broken bones
and a badly damaged face, she was soon on
the way to recovery. The surgeons performed
miracles, making her face recognisable again.

During this time, Moyra knew she was
in God's hands and was very aware of prayer
support from those around her. She asked
God only for courage and strength to cope.

Despite her progress, Moyra felt that
she had let her husband down. She would
no longer be able to groom the bulls and
her husband had also injured himself in
coming to her rescue. But her reading of
Colossians 1 reminded her that she was not
called upon to be successful, only faithful.
Some words from 2 Corinthians also helped
her greatly. 'Praise be to the God ... of all
comfort, who comforts us in all our troubles,
so that we can comfort those in any trouble
with the comfort we ourselves have received
from God' (2 Corinthians 1:3–4, NIV).

This was borne out by those who visited Moyra in hospital. Staff and patients alike told of how she uplifted everyone's spirits The ward sister commented to the doctor that Moyra brought 'new life' to the ward.

Because of her injuries, she was propped up in bed each morning to wash herself. She could move only her arms, and it was quite an effort, but she found it helpful to sing quietly some well-known hymns and songs of praise. She was so thankful to be alive and so aware of God's presence. Indeed, one of the other patients had a hymn book brought in so that she could join in with Moyra. Many patients came to share their faith as well as their fears and doubts.

Moyra's own fear came when she was discharged from hospital with the words of an elderly patient ringing in her ears: 'Get away home and get on with your life! You have things to do. Find out what they are'.

The accident may have affected those Moyra loved most – as well as herself – but she was to discover that they too were to be strengthened in the months ahead.

Despite the pain and discomfort, Moyra has experienced the uplifting hand of God in her life. Finding out what her tasks were to be has not always been easy. Listening instead of doing, sewing instead of rushing around – at times she struggles with feel-

ings of letting God down, being inade-
quate by not being able to do so much due
to her injuries.

Moyra's advice to us all would be to
forget ourselves, and rest in the Lord,
reminding us of the words of Hebrews 11:
'Now faith is being sure of what we hope
for and certain of what we do not see' (NIV).

~ MEG STEWART ~

EFFIE
CAMPBELL

'OUR EFFIE!'

'Our Effie!' – but *whose* Effie is she? EFFIE
is a daughter of Glasgow, living most of her
life in Cathcart, on the south-side of the
city. She was raised in a church-going family
– it was her grandmother who took
her to that particular Salvation
Army meeting at which the
nine year old Effie went forward and gave her life to Jesus.
On returning home, her father
reminded her of the undertaking which lay ahead – from
then on, before doing anything, she
must decide if it was something Jesus
would wish her to do. Henceforth, Effie's life
was centred around the church, particularly
Cathcart South Church, and she speaks
fondly of her days in the Girls' Association.

EFFIE
CAMPBELL

At 29, she married George Campbell,
looking forward eagerly to starting a family.
But George was dogged by ill-health and it
seemed increasingly unlikely. Effie took this
set-back with her usual common sense –
'Better to have a husband and no children,

than no husband' – and looked for an alternative outlet for their love of children. Their home was a wonderful place for their friends' children and Effie concentrated on working with the young people in the church.

At the age of 39, Effie herself became unwell. As she said, 'the germ she had took feet!' and she gave birth to a long-awaited child – a baby girl they called Elspeth.

But, only a few years later George developed Alzheimers' disease. Effie cared for him until his death. Widowed at 48, she found herself searching for a new challenge in life – this time back to school to get the qualifications she had missed out on in her youth. With the help of friends, she attended classes in the evenings and eventually gained her Higher Certificate.

Thoughts of the ministry were not in Effie's mind, but friends persuaded her that, given her previous church service, perhaps she was being called to the Kirk's ministry – or, as Effie said, either 'shoved or led'. So she became the Revd Effie Campbell BD.

Then she became 'Cumnock's Effie' – applying for the vacant charge of Crichton West in the town of Cumnock in Ayrshire at the age of 59. But, sorry to say, they didn't want her – she was a woman! However, the vacancy committee of Crichton West did go and listen to her preach which resulted in Effie being invited to preach as sole nominee. As sole nominee, she had to conduct Sunday worship before the whole congregation, thus allowing them to come to a decision about whether to appoint her.

On that day the folk in Crichton West were still not happy about the prospect of a 'woman minister' in their Kirk. But, regardless, Effie fell for Crichton West in a big way – literally so, since at the end of the service she fell down the pulpit steps! No doubt it was her wonderful Glasgow sense of humour which won their votes at the end of the day. For the last hymn contained the line, 'If e'er I disown thee I stumble and fall'! Effie Campbell was elected *unanimously*!

The Cumnock folk grew to love 'their Effie' so much that she was not allowed to retire at 65. When she finally bade farewell in 1991, they honoured her with their love and affection. At her final service, they stood as she entered the pulpit, and at the Benediction they sang to her, 'The Lord bless thee, and keep thee'.

'Retirement' for Effie meant a move to the lovely seaside town of Ayr. Now she is 'Ayr's Effie' and working as hard as ever at whatever she is called upon to do.

Glasgow's Effie? Cumnock's Effie? Ayr's Effie? But certainly God's Effie.

~ HELEN W BURNS ~

ISABEL
STEWART

A GOOD NEIGHBOUR

There is a lady in our village of Strathmiglo
who has made a very deep impression on me.
I've known **Mrs ISABEL STEWART** for over
twenty years. She is a regular church-goer
and guildswoman and she is well known
for the many kindnesses she shows. When
she bakes for her family or for a function,
there are always a few extra items for the
elderly or infirm staying nearby. When
there's a power cut, there's always soup and
tea for those in all-electric homes.

Isabel Stewart has brought up her family
of three daughters and one son to be honest
trustworthy adults. And for nine years she
nursed her husband through motor-
neurone disease. Although George Stewart
was not helpless all that time, he needed
everything done for him in the last three
years of his life. He was nursed at home with
only a few brief respite stays in hospital.

What impressed us all was the loving,
uncomplaining way Isabel coped, continuing to give George his place as head of the
house, even when he could no longer speak.

Following her husband's death, Isabel moved house, but she still keeps an eye on former neighbours and is always ready to help others.

We know Isabel as someone who never for one moment imagines that she has done, or is, anything special. She never speaks ill of anyone, but always looks for the good. To my mind, she is a good example of a person living out her Christian beliefs wherever she is.

~ PEGGY MATTHEW ~

KIRSTY
GIBSON

'Aye fleein' aboot!'

You could say that life began again for
KIRSTY GIBSON (née SEMPLE) when she
became 57. Crucial to this new beginning
were the prayers of a group of women in
Kinross.

The year was 1981. Kirsty had been a
doctor in a Dundee general practice for the
previous thirty years. It was said frequently
and appreciatively by her many patients
that Kirsty gave herself to her medical work,
meaning that she shared her immense compassion and energy, her delightful humour
and her lively Christian faith, without stint.
Kirsty, however, would be the first to say
that if she had a lot to give, it was because
she had received so much – especially from
a very wise, loving, resilient and faithful
mother.

In the early years of Kirsty's life at
Lauriston Place in Edinburgh, her mother
hoped that her wee girl would commit
herself to Christ *and* that she would train as
a doctor. Kirsty sealed the former at a
Scripture Union camp at Nairn. Later, she

accomplished her medical training at Surgeon's Hall, Edinburgh in 1946.

The forward momentum of Kirsty's faith, life and work threatened to come to a shuddering halt in 1981 when she was told that she was suffering from a critical narrowing of the carotid arteries, and was advised to stop working immediately and live a quiet life.

The day after receiving this news, Kirsty was due to speak to the Woman's Guild in Kinross. Upon hearing of her plight, the women present prayed earnestly for her. The next day, one member telephoned Kirsty suggesting that she read Psalm 116 in the Good News Bible. There she found the words: 'I am your servant, Lord; I serve you just as my mother did. You have saved me from death'.

Encouraged by this, Kirsty called several people over to her house, including her minister Jock Stein of the Steeple Church, a Pentecostal pastor, an Episcopal and a Roman Catholic priest, a Jewish Christian and some other close friends. On the basis of James 5:14, these 'elders' prayed for her and anointed her with oil. At that point, she knew in herself that she was physically healed. Shortly afterward, she found satisfactory medical treatment for a depressive illness which had troubled her over the years.

Although Kirsty left general practice, it was not to live the recommended quiet life! Instead she threw herself into the service of her Lord in a variety of new directions. She was now free to develop her ministry alongside persons and families afflicted by alcohol and drug abuse. She later became involved with folk devastated by the onset of AIDS. She is now associated with the Health and Healing Group of Dundee Presbytery and with a mastectomy support group. She and a close friend are also faithful and frequent prison visitors.

Although her help is called upon by many individuals and groups within the church and outside it, she invariably finds the time to respond positively to any situation. Kirsty may be 'aye fleein' aboot' – as she puts it – yet her life is wonderfully led by the Spirit. She has known, and continues to know, personal sadness, yet she gladly identifies with the words: 'Praise, my soul, the King of heaven … ransomed, healed, restored, forgiven, who like me his praise should sing!'

~ GRAHAM FOSTER ~

SUSAN

Following JESUS

I first met SUSAN when she dropped out of university in a state of nervous collapse, brought on by difficulties at home with an alcoholic father. At that time, Susan met some young people who had given their lives to God. She was attracted by their freedom of heart and zest for living and decided to experiment with their ideas – after all, when you feel that others need to change, the best place to start is with yourself.

By applying Jesus' teachings about purity, unselfishness and honesty, Susan faced up to where she had fallen far short of his standards and claimed forgiveness. As she began to find the freedom she longed for, a new love for her father grew.

Susan once said to me that, whereas her psychiatrist seemed to point her to someone else to blame for her troubles, Jesus left her in no doubt about her own responsibility for them. With this more positive frame of mind, she went back to her studies and she has now graduated, passing on her own experiences of Jesus Christ to her friends.

~ MARGARET GLEN ~

ANN
REID

NEW LIFE

At the tender age of two and a half, ANN REID, with her father, mother and older brother, moved to East Kilbride in Lanarkshire. Everything around her, as she grew up here, was *new*: schools, church, house, shops, fresh bright play area and safe roads. Being part of a Christian family brought Ann quickly into the life of the church.

Ann studied at Robert Gordon's College in Aberdeen, obtaining her degree in 1977. In the following year she gained the State Registration Diploma in Dietetics. However, unable to find work in Scotland, Ann found herself a job in Belfast.

She always says that these three years in Northern Ireland formed the real basis of her future career: 'I learned so much from my colleagues, professionally and personally, from the struggles they had faced for so long ... yet their cheerfulness was infectious and their hospitality crossed barriers

ANN REID

the media could never even imagine'.

In 1981 Ann returned to Glasgow to work as a Health Education Officer in Nutrition, returning to her own home and family. Within the church family of Westwood, she became a Sunday School teacher, member of the Congregational Board and an Elder. She was also active on the local committee of the National Bible Society. But, all this time, Ann knew within her heart there was something else she wanted to do.

Ann's father died in 1986 and, with her deep faith and commitment to her work, when given the opportunity to go to St Colm's College to train, she accepted the invitation, knowing, at last, what she wanted to do with her life. For, in 1988 Ann was appointed missionary to serve with the Presbyterian Church of Ghana as a Nutritionist/Tutor of the Nurses Training College, Agogo Hospital – an answer to her prayers of many years to work in a developing country.

Warmly welcomed by the Agogo people, and settling into her newly-decorated flat, Ann eagerly awaited her first 'day'. That day begins at 5 am! It was normal practice to attend church at this early hour before setting off for work – to thank God for the night's rest and to ask him to be with you during the day ahead. As Ann lived and worked with her Ghanaian friends, and colleagues from other countries, she appreciated even more what it meant to depend on God for everything – rain, to replenish low water supplies; hope, when healing seemed impossible; courage, to go on praying even when answers do not seem to be forthcoming.

Living alongside people who put their faith into action has been a great source of strength and inspiration to Ann. She herself has inspired others, through her work and compassion in sometimes very difficult situations. All of them together radiate God's love in action with a smile, a greeting, and through their caring.

As a child, Ann faced a new life in East Kilbride; as a woman she faces a new life in Agogo – to teach in the college and work in the hospital, serving with Christian faith and love.

~ BARBARA HERRON ~

WINNIE

speaking for GOD!

You would pass **WINNIE** in the street and hardly notice her. A small unassuming woman in her mid 70s, you will not find her at the centre of things – organising, tea-making or dashing from committee to committee.

Winnie's first husband died during World War II. Later, with her second husband and her children, she moved to Scotland, to the small town where she now lives, determined to make a new life. But at first, she found it hard to adjust. After all, she grew up in a comfortable Anglican household in Yorkshire. Scotland must have seemed very different to her.

Through the ups and downs of the years that followed, Winnie's mind was always active in her search for God. Ordination as an elder, and a stint as Guild president followed in the early 1970s. After that she appeared to take more of a back seat, although she continued to read and think about God, and contribute regular pieces on prayer to the church magazine.

Winnie was asked to help in a Guild service during Holy Week in 1990. Despite a life-long stammer (which sadly denied her the prospect of higher education) which becomes more noticeable when Winnie is nervous, her address was excellent – well researched, thoughtful, thought-provoking. Since then she has preached at Guild dedications, Holy Week services and at the 1992 New Year service, which came soon after her husband's death. On that occasion, she spoke very movingly about 'Time'. The hesitation in speech and manner is still there, but the power of her faith in God speaks volumes.

So don't pass Winnie by in the street. She walks with God.

~ CAROL HERBERT ~

HELEN
GREIG

SHARING *after* SUFFERING

It has been a great privilege to share stories
of faith with Guild members – all of which
left their mark on my own life. However, on
my travels, I met HELEN GREIG whose story
made a great impression on me.

Helen was born in Kirkintilloch, but
moved to Irvine and then to Newton
Mearns, where she and her sister went to
Hutcheson's Grammar School, Glasgow.
They were brought up in a family where,
with her father an elder, the Christian faith
was central to their lives.

In her teenage years, Helen went through
a period of doubt and uncertainty. Indeed it
wasn't until she was married, and her son
Stuart was born, that she thought seriously
again about her own faith and re-discovered
its meaning for her own life. She remembers
well sharing with a friend how difficult it
would be to believe in a loving God, if she
were ever to lose her own child.

When Stuart was two and a half, Helen
was blessed with twins – Lynsey and Martin
– two beautiful, normal babies who brought

great joy to their parents and friends. The family soon settled into a new routine and were quite unprepared for the horror which befell them three months later when Martin died, a victim of cot death.

Why should this perfectly healthy and normal baby die in this way? Helen recounted her thoughts of previous years and now affirms that this tragedy, far from driving her away from her faith in a loving God, brought him closer and made his presence much more of a reality for her. She was always aware of the presence of Christ carrying her through the times of heartache and the coming to terms with her grief. In addition, she was upheld and uplifted by the prayers of family and friends, not least her husband Tony.

Helen kept a record of her feelings and emotions from day to day, as she learned to cope with one toddler and one small baby instead of two. Her diary of these difficult months has been a great blessing to others facing similar experiences. Helen has spoken to many groups of parents whose heartache at losing a child she can so readily understand. Indeed, her willingness to share her faith, as it helped her through this ordeal, is a great inspiration.

~ DOROTHY DALGLIESH ~

HELEN DAWSON *

The WISE VIRGIN

If ever there walked and talked one who understood that God's work must be done by God's people in God's way by God's power, HELEN DAWSON was one of those folk. This is her story.

Helen was the eldest of eight children, born into a humble home in Banffshire. Her father was a gate-crossing attendant and railway linesman. His wages never exceeded one pound per week and he augmented this with vegetables grown on the embankment, and with coal that dropped off passing trains. He died in early middle age, poor in the world's goods, but rich in faith. Helen became the breadwinner for the family.

Before this, at 13, Helen had heard an itinerant preacher speak on the parable of the wise and foolish virgins. She ran back as fast as she could to her house so that she could begin straight away to give her all to God. In that single decisive act of dedication, the seed of becoming a missionary was sown and she set about studying hard to prepare for university.

But, at her father's death, it was clear to Helen where her duty lay – to her mother, brothers and sisters. She found immediate employment as a pupil teacher while she studied for full teaching status. With a small salary and educational grant, she accepted the responsibility of the family budget until her brothers and sisters were grown up. Her mother certainly had no occasion to want over her long years – Helen was a strong channel of spiritual and material support.

Although denied overseas adventure, Helen invested her hopes where it pleased God. Over the forty years she tutored as teacher and headmistress, she won the affection and appreciation of her pupils. She was to keep contact with many of them – her 'bairns'. However, at sixty, with family priorities no longer her direct concern, Helen retired to pursue the deferred missionary attraction of younger years.

But *where* and *how*? Persistent prayer led her to Aberdeen where she shared her hopes with a greatly respected minister called Alexander Frazer. Listening very carefully, he prayed earnestly with her. Then he said, 'My dear, you are too old to go abroad as a missionary. I am sure there is much you can and will do here for the Lord'. Suddenly Helen realised that everyone outside of Christ was a mission field, and that in God's eyes there was no distinction between 'home' or 'foreign' venture. To be a missionary was to go where Christ was not. And so her marching orders slowly crystallised.

Looking round the parish, Helen found a large flax mill employing women from very humble homes, with limited learning. She sought permission to enter the mill and soon her cheery attitude won the confidence and friendship of the women. She was able to sift out what help she could give them.

In time, Helen invited the women to the church hall, where she taught them craft skills, household hints and cookery. Some were taught to read and write. Like Topsy, the range of projects just grew and grew.

It was inevitable that Helen added a spiritual dimension to all that she did. A study of women of the Bible led to a Bible class which in turn became the nucleus of the fellowship.

In later years, Helen became captive to arthritis. Housebound, moving only from chair to chair, she still pursued her life of devotion and service. She could read, she could write, she could pray.

Helen had cast her bread upon the waters over many years and the returning tide brought love and comfort from those she had loved. They visited, wrote, telephoned.

Her prayers of gratitude led to further

work for God. The daily newspaper, with its intimations of 'Hatches, Matches and Despatches', provided a way to a rarely used ministry – intercession. Helen began a mission that confirmed to her the power of prayer. What she sought for those she prayed for, only God and Helen knew. But, with her prayers went little gifts and cards of good wishes or condolence – especially for the bereaved. Those of her friends who knew what she was doing donated some of the gifts and cards she sent out.

She further began to pray for those in prison and made enquiries of the police about families of prisoners to whom she sent gifts and money. School children, mill workers and members of the congregation all helped with donations. Even those working overseas sent foreign currency which Helen's minister exchanged for her.

Now over ninety, Helen continued to pray. Those who gathered with her when she was near to death recall how she added her assent to the last prayer she made with the words, 'Amen! Amen! Amen!'.

Helen's faith made things possible for her and her love made things easy. She was a wise virgin whose lamp was fuelled by an eternal light.

[*Compiled by Marjorie Lawrie from material submitted by Peggy Birkbeck.*]

AUNT
ETHEL

An EXAMPLE *to* FOLLOW!

When we were asked to write about someone who had influenced our lives, I pushed
the thought to the back of my mind.
Recently, however, I remembered **Aunt
Ethel**.

I had been brought up in a Christian
home. Throughout my life there had always
been someone there who was interested in
my church work – that person was my
father's sister, Aunt Ethel.

She taught in the local primary school,
which I attended. Each morning, we would
walk along to school together. She always
looked smart. Heads would turn and folk
would acknowledge her. She was a much-
respected lady. Indeed, she had probably
taught them and their families, written
references for them, visited them when they
were ill, helped them when they were in
trouble – generally taken an interest in
their welfare.

A devout Christian, Aunt Ethel had
dreams of going to China as a missionary,
but she was the breadwinner at home. She

even sold her college medals to help her sick brother after the War.

As church elder and treasurer, Aunt Ethel had a particular interest in young people. On our walks together, she taught me the names of wild flowers and showed me where the birds nested every year. She encouraged me to read her books, many of which had been school prizes, and this lead to my reading a good deal of poetry. One particular book, *Chalk Talks for the Young*, contained illustrations of white chalk on a black background. At night, I still remember many of the biblical texts quoted in this book.

Aunt Ethel followed my nursing career with great interest and was always ready to listen to my problems and anxieties. When I married, this interest extended to my husband and family, and to all that I was involved in.

She was, quite simply, a lovely lady – full of wisdom, truth, concern and love. I keep trying to live up to her example.

~ ANNE CUNNINGHAM ~

ANNE
DAWSON

FIVE HATS

Born in 1955, a native of Clackmannan,
ANNE DAWSON was educated at Alloa
Academy and Edinburgh University. She
became a teacher of chemistry at Lornshill
Academy, Alloa, where she made friends
with parents, children and teachers alike.

Anne made the decision to go to St
Colm's College, Edinburgh and, on
completion of her training in 1976, she
was appointed head teacher at the Robert
Laws Secondary School at Embangweni,
Malawi. It was here that she learned to be a
jack-of-all-trades, wearing five hats.

The first hat was worn for administra-
tion and teaching, working toward good
examination results, and care for all the
girls she taught. The second hat was worn
for maintenance – in this case, concern for
the school water supply, not something
many teachers have to worry about. Water
barrels had to be maintained in the various
catchment areas. Anne's third hat was worn
for oversight of the kitchen and gardens –
the latter a vital source of food supply. She

had to learn about planting seeds and the growing seasons. The fourth hat was one few of us might wish to wear – maintenance of a diesel engine. Spare parts took time to arrive, so Ann had to learn the hard way about how to carry out repairs. The fifth and final hat meant responsibility for the transport of supplies to the rural schools, some of which were many miles away. In the rainy season, the roads became quagmires of mud which made travelling very difficult, if not impossible.

In 1991, Jenifer Barrett, a member of the Woman's Guild in Killearn back in Scotland, visited Anne and spent a month in Malawi with her. She was given a very hospitable welcome and Anne made her feel at home. Jenifer found Anne to be a very practical person, loyal to those who genuinely wanted the good of the school and very direct in her dealings with everyone.

Of Anne, Jenifer notes that she prefers to be sent on a welding course during her furlough, rather than spend time at St Colm's. She also notes that Anne has a very dry sense of humour; that she is fun to be with, but takes her work very seriously indeed – her success at the Robert Laws school was the reason for her transfer to Ekwendeni.

Anne is also a keen photographer and enjoys sport – she is a former Scottish hockey internationalist. She is an excellent cook and baker – in all, a multi-talented lady who uses her gifts for the good of others.

Through the Partner Plan, Anne is in touch with a few churches in Scotland. One of these is Tillicoultry, and her furlough visits are much enjoyed. She spends time with the Sunday school children, who are often amazed by the stories that Anne has to tell. The children have come to realise how fortunate they are, compared to their African counterparts – and willingly collect money to buy pencils and rubbers for Anne to take back to Africa.

When she is far away from home, Anne appreciates a copy of her local newspaper. Once read, it is used in the kiln fire to bake the mud bricks which are then used to build wells and houses.

Anne has now moved on to become head teacher of Ekwendeni Girls' School. She is a tireless worker in God's name, bringing love and honour into all things at all times. She is an inspiration to all who know her – a modern woman of faith

~ JEAN POLLOCK *and* MARJORIE LAWRIE ~

MARGARET
McMILLAN

PIONEER *or* PROPHET?

MARGARET MCMILLAN [1860–1931] was born of Scottish parents in New York on 20th July 1860. She sprang from an ancestry Highland, mystic, Protestant, Catholic, with a family motto 'I learn to succour the helpless'.

Margaret was educated in the capital of the Highlands – Inverness – where it is said the best English is spoken. She was sent to finishing school in Switzerland and first earned her living as a governess. By her own account this was the period of her life when her childhood faith became alive. Through a religious experience she saw herself to be 'the instrument of the unseen'.

By 1888 Margaret was living in London with her sister Rachel. While there, a titled lady was impressed by Margaret's striking appearance and excellent voice and paid for her to have a course of stage training.

Margaret worked hard all this time, teaching music to groups of factory girls and continuing her extensive reading of literature on education, philosophy and sociology. It was her belief that she had to use her gifts in the service of education.

In those days, when many children had little or no schooling at all, her approach to education was not only intellectual, but practical. Her conviction was derived from her Christianity and philosophy, as well as her social conscience and political bias.

In 1894, a year after taking up an appointment with the new Independent Labour Party, Margaret won a place on a Bradford school board. It was here that she campaigned for the numerous, dirty and undernourished children of the town. She also arranged for the first-ever medical inspection of school children.

Her knowledge of music and voice production made her aware of the prevalence of faulty breathing habits among the children and so she campaigned by writing and distributing a pamphlet to their mothers. Then she worked to get school baths installed, meals and clinics, while at the same time researching into the relationship between mental and physical health.

The works of many famous educationalists, including Edouard Séguin, a French pioneer in the education of mentally retarded children, inspired her to write her main book on educational theory, *Education through the Imagination.*

However, it was her work with the
Bradford children which was to influence
her for the next thirty years.

In 1903, Margaret McMillan returned
to London to join her sister, Rachel, in plan-
ning a health centre. She published papers
at this time and for the next ten years the
two sisters founded many clinics, remedial
centres, camps for schoolchildren, not to
mention starting an open-air nursery school
in Deptford in 1911.

Margaret always stressed that only when
the health of the child from birth has been
recognised as a basic human responsibility
and community concern, can the other aims
of education be sought with any prospect of
success. Sadly some of the children who
Margaret came across had no early experience of love, beauty and play to give them
the primary development of feelings.

Parents and others were becoming
interested in nursery schools for children
under the age of five. In 1923, when a
Nursery Schools Association was formed,
Margaret McMillan was chosen to be the
first president, having already in 1917
received the CBE in recognition of her great
services to education.

She believed that many of the learning
and behavioural difficulties in young
children would remedy themselves if only

the children were physically and mentally well cared for, aiming at the free and full development of the intellect and personality of the individual. To achieve this there should be no deprived children in the community. Thus began child health and infant teaching irrespective of their social standing in the community.

Despite all the difficulties of the time, Margaret McMillan kept striving for what she believed to be right. The belief in the creative power of the mind was, in her view, the quality every human being should be able to develop and use in their personal life and work.

Margaret McMillan has been described as mystic, emotional, practical, intellectual – both scholar and saint. She herself asserted that the real source of her power was spiritual.

~ CARYL A DAVIDSON ~

MARY
SLESSOR

Pushing back the DARKNESS

I used to hear about her from my grandmother, who recalled her as a young woman.
But **MARY SLESSOR** [1848–1915] was no
ordinary young woman. Her destiny lay far
from the clacking machinery of the
jute factory where she, like hundreds of other Dundee women,
toiled the twelve-hour day.

Impoverished by the
ruinous habits of a drunken
father, the Slessor family knew
nothing but struggle. Yet through
the drabness of their lives there
shone like a beacon, the strong Christian
faith of their mother.

MARY
SLESSOR

A woman of piety and refinement, Mary's
mother saw to it that her boys and girls
(seven in all) were regular in attendance at
Wishart Church and Sunday School. Deeply
interested in Foreign Missions, and well-
read in the subject, Mrs Slessor would tell
her children of the dark, heathen lands
across the seas awaiting the coming of the
light of knowledge.

She talked a great deal about Calabar, and it was her dream that one of her two sons should become a missionary. This dream ended sadly with the early deaths of the two boys. It was then that a spark was kindled in Mary Slessor. Could she be the one to fulfil her mother's dearest wish?

It was not easy. Working in the factory, teaching in Sunday School, reading avidly to educate herself, Mary, the main support of the family after her father's death, waited 14 years. Then, seeing home circumstances somewhat improved, she offered herself to the Foreign Mission Board.

She asked to be sent to Calabar, on the west coast of Africa: dangerous, disease-ridden Nigeria, known as the White Man's Grave!

In that year of 1876, Mary Slessor was 28, red-haired, with a fiery spirit to match. Her strong conviction that this was the work she was meant to do carried her through the first difficult period of her service in the main Mission Station in Duke Town. Growing restless there, she became convinced her real challenge lay farther away, in the interior, amongst the benighted, savage tribes of the bush lands.

Granted official permission at last, she penetrated far into the forests, bravely stifling her fear of the jungle animals, the

sinister reptiles. Eventually she reached the
territory of the wild Okoyong tribe. Here,
she felt, was work waiting for her to do.

To deepen her understanding of these
terrifying people, Mary decided she must
live as one of them, in a mud hut, walk
barefoot, eat their kind of food, learn their
difficult language. And face their bitter
hostility.

Witchcraft, twin murder and drunken-
ness were a way of life for the Okoyong.
Buttressed by her tremendous faith in the
power of prayer, and seeking guidance
constantly from her well-thumbed bible,
Mary battled on in her lonely, Herculean
task. She rescued numberless babies, faced
up to angry tribal chiefs (often wielding her
trusty umbrella to good effect) and treated
ailments with the medical skills she had
learned in Duke Town.

Her single-handed achievements were
enormous. But the treacherous climate
gradually wore down her physical
resistance. She would return home on
furlough, drained and exhausted from
bouts of fever. When asked to speak at
meetings in Scotland, she became paralysed
with nerves. She would far rather have had
a confrontation with an irate tribal chief!
And always she was impatient to return to
Calabar, to the abandoned children she

had fostered and trained. Her 'bairns'.

Mary Slessor became a living legend. Her missionary work was spreading, transforming the lives of countless people in the territory she had made her own. The spark which had been kindled in a grey Dundee tenement had blazed into a glorious life of service and self-sacrifice. Her dedication had pushed back the darkness in the savage lands she served, letting in the healing light of the Gospel.

But her health was wrecked. After heroic struggles against illness, she died in the winter of 1915, worn out at the age of 67. The 'Mother of All the Peoples' died on station, surrounded by her faithful 'children' and mourned by thousands.

My grandmother's story was a more conventional one. But, just for a short time, her life had touched that of one singled out and set aside to do great things and work wonders in dark and perilous places.

~ WINIFRED NICOLSON ~

The
UNSUNG
MEMBERS

The women who have been written about in this book are included for a variety of reasons. Some are well known; others are known only to a very few people. They all have one thing in common – they made a deep impact on others by the faith which was and is the basis of their lives.

And so it is with many women in the Guild. The following contribution sums up so well the real strength of our organisation – the faith and the commitment of the individual members.

Mrs Lilias Twaddle of West Kilbride, St Andrews, wrote to us:

'The other week I attended a meeting of our local Woman's Guild. The ladies are a happy crowd, all well-known to one another.

'After the opening prayer and hymn, the President began the business part of the meeting. She asked for someone to write a letter to the headquarters of the Guild about any outstanding ladies known to the members. My name was mentioned to do just that. "But *all* the ladies are outstanding," I replied. This caused much laughter, but I meant what I said.

'I know, as we all do, that many wonderful women are Guild members. Throughout my sojourn in Scotland, I have been a member of a number of churches. No matter where I have travelled, there have always been wonderful women in this organisation. They have spent their lives doing things for others, especially those in need. Much money has been handed over to church authorities and not once have I heard a grumble. It has always been considered a privilege to be able to help others in our Lord's name. Over the years, this attitude of thanksgiving has remained.

'So who was I to say which lady was more famous than another from among all these happy women. They live a caring and sharing existence for their community. What would the Church and the Guild do without the unsung members? The Lord bless them all.'